Someday A Blessing

Deborah Raney and Denise Raney Thompson

PublishAmerica
Baltimore

© 2005 by Deborah Raney and Denise Raney Thompson. All rights reserved. No part of this book may be reproduced, stored in a retrieval system or transmitted in any form or by any means without the prior written permission of the publishers, except by a reviewer who may quote brief passages in a review to be printed in a newspaper, magazine or journal.

First printing

ISBN: 1-4137-4954-2
PUBLISHED BY PUBLISHAMERICA, LLLP
www.publishamerica.com
Baltimore

Printed in the United States of America

Dedication

Mom,
We would like to thank you for taking care of us for all those
years. Your tears at night never fell unheard. We dedicate this book
to you with love, respect, and honor. We are so proud to have you as
our mother. We love you, Mom.
Your daughters,
Deborah and Denise

Special Dedication

We would also like to make a special dedication of this book to
our grandparents Frank and Veronica Stanski. Although we never
had the pleasure of meeting you, your voices call out to us from the
streets of heaven. We have only come to know you through our
mothers' eyes. We know you through her sense of humor, her laughter,
her bravery, and all her hopes and dreams. We look forward to the
day when we can touch and hold you and never part.
Love, your granddaughters,
Deborah and Denise

Acknowledgments

We want to thank all of our friends and family members who showed their support during the writing of this book. Denise gives a special thanks to her best friend Veronica Smith Schaberg for encouraging her for years to complete this project. Eleanore Heuer, thanks so much for helping to put the final touches on our story. Your encouragement and kind words are so appreciated.

Prologue

Her face cradled in her hands. She cried tears of disbelief, even though she knew this day was coming. The letters threatening repossession of the furniture were becoming a reality. She sat on an old wooden fold-up chair that the Sheriff brought up from the basement. Her eyes were a blur. She looked around at the now empty living room. A brilliant shaft of sunlight stabs through the window illuminating the floating dust motes. Family pictures once displayed neatly with pride were now lying on the floor; knick-knacks were scattered along the baseboards by the seemingly uncaring repo men. The bedroom she once shared with the love of her life now only contained her undergarments, lying in disorganized piles. The three-bedroom home was now hollow and emptied in just two hours. Only marks left on the floors remained from the five years of happiness that once existed there.

Sophie stood a mere 5'4", sandy blonde hair, eyes a cool mint green with a petite, rounded face. She had a beautiful smile and a contagious laugh. Her sense of humor caught the attention of many. Sophie dressed impeccably, wearing crisply pressed skirts and colorful, form-fitting knit sweaters. She loved the fact she could now wear lipstick, something she never had in Poland. Red was her favorite color. Seamed stockings accented her shapely legs and high-heeled shoes only helped to define their toned beauty. Sophie was very proud of all of her accomplishments up until now.

She once had a handsome family, a brand-new home, new Ford Station Wagon, and a speedboat to pull to the lake on weekends. The home was furnished with all new furniture, a wringer washer and a clothes line out in the plush green fenced backyard. The children were happy and enjoyed playing with their pets, a black cat they called Midnight and a Shepard/Collie mix they named Tippy. Her life was all anyone could ask for. She was living the All-American Dream.

Now, she sat in an empty living room on the wooden fold-up chair as she tried to compose herself before her four children. The children knelt beside her on the living room floor while she stared long and hard at the truck where the men were preparing to haul her life away. The truck reminded her of the one that took her away many years ago, away from her family in Poland. She's walked down this road before, alone, frightened with fearful thoughts of what the future would hold.

She cried to herself, burying her face even deeper into her cupped hands. *Please let this all be a bad dream, please, God!*

Her children move closer to her in an effort to comfort their mother as only children know how. Sophie couldn't hold the tears back. Everything is gone. Her life has been shattered once again and Sophie cried silently.

I don't know what to tell them. How can I keep them now? She clenched her eyes tighter as her thoughts trailed off to all the disconnection notices that crammed her mailbox daily.

Her tears went unnoticed by all the strangers that have invaded her home that day, carrying away her hopes and dreams. Helplessly, she sat surrounded by four children: Daryl, 10; David, 8; Deborah, 6; and Denise, 4. Men were once again re-writing another dark chapter in her life.

Sophie's next door neighbors, Lonnie and Chuck, offered to take her children for the night. As Sophie escorted the children out the front door, she noticed other neighbors standing in their yards or on

SOMEDAY A BLESSING

the porches of their homes, watching her humiliation and the destruction of her family. All of her neighbors had watched Sophie's marriage fall apart before their eyes, and some even helped in its destruction. Some neighbors would wait with food and furniture to give her, while others sat back, proud of their participation in that destruction. As the children reluctantly walked next door, it only brought on a greater feeling of loneliness and helplessness. Sophie turned and walked back inside the now-empty house and sat down on the wooden chair. Her footsteps echoed back at her from the hollow confines of the house. The chair squeaked with her weight as she sat down. Sophie now sat alone in an empty home that was once filled with laughter. Dinner was always ready on the table for her husband; the kids crowded by the door to run out and greet him when he arrived. The house was maintained spotless, all clothes ironed, and patios swept clean daily.

I've worked so hard, she thought, *for nothing, all for nothing! Just so that bitch could take it all away! I can't believe this! Not again. I was so happy, so very happy.* She cried aloud.

As she lay on one of the two single beds she had begged to keep for her children, Sophie drifted off into a restless sleep, her mind racing with thoughts.

Why couldn't I make him happy? I did everything for that man! I never should have walked down that street that day. I don't think I can do this. I can't take this anymore!

She soon succumbed to a much-needed slumber. The next morning, Sophie was unable to get herself to rise out of bed. With her eyes open, she lay for hours, staring at the ceiling, knowing her four children were next door. She was not ready to face them. She was not ready to even attempt to explain the previous day's events, nor could she find the words that her children could even begin to understand. She began reminiscing of the happier times when she was a little girl and about all the events in her life that had lead her to America. In the midst of tears and tissues, Sophie tenderly recalled the day that she and her sister Stasia went to have their fortunes told in Poznan, Poland.

9

Chapter One
A Place in the Heart

Nine-year-old Sophie sat down at the table. She could not help but stare into the gypsy's face at a table draped with colorful cloth remnants of reds and yellows. Her long hair lay coarsely along her slender shoulders, pulled back off her face with a self-made bandana. Her eyes were deep set and dark. Sophie thought how the gypsy's face showed more years than she had probably lived.

Her voice was tranquil as she told Sophie, "I see here that you will cross great waters someday. There will also be two dark-haired men in your life." The gypsy leaned closer over the table and quietly spoke again. "One you will love forever, another will have wealth!"

Sophie asked quietly, "Will I have children?"

The gypsy whispered softly, "Yes, little one. I see four, four in your future, two boys and two girls. That's all I have to say."

"Great waters? Me?!" Sophie laughed as she and Stasia ran out the door, leaning on one another for their brisk walk home. As the day's end drew near, Sophie could not rid herself of the words the gypsy spoke. She couldn't imagine traveling any further than Poznan.

Times were hard in pre-war Poland. The world was slowly recovering from the Great Depression of 1929. Political unrest was occurring in Germany. Spain was experiencing internal strife, also.

11

In an effort to provide for his family, Sophie's father Frank left his family and went to Holland to find work. He would write to his wife and send her money each time he wrote. Sophie's mother, Veronica, anxiously waited for each letter from Frank. She had received many before, but this one would be the one that would reunite the family with him in Holland.

The Stanki's had lived in a small four room apartment on the second floor. The stairs came to a landing where there was a huge window overlooking the streets of Poznan. Around the corner, a few feet further was the apartment door. The kids shared one bedroom and Frank and Veronica had their own. A small arched door led into a quaint kitchen off a small entryway where they hung their winter coats on nails and kicked off their shoes. The kitchen was small, with only a few cupboards to pack enough food for a family of six. The walls were white, with many cracks to show the apartment's age. A wooden square table was placed in the corner where they would have to take turns to eat. It was too small to seat the whole family together. Veronica cooked on a red brick stove that was built into the corner wall that used coal. Sophie loved the kitchen and liked leaning on the cupboard shelf watching her mother cook, smelling the food as it was being removed from the stove to cool. A small closet off the kitchen held their smoked meats that Veronica would buy at the market. Sophie recalled seeing her father cutting off chunks of meat for a snack, some of which were molded. She could not believe her father would eat moldy meat, but in their house, there wasn't an option if one was hungry. It disgusted her.

Life was simple, but far from easy, for the Stanskis. They had neither an icebox, nor an inside bathroom or running water. All baths were taken in the kitchen in a large wash tub with heated water poured from a bucket by their mother. Oil lamps lit their way through the evening hours. Veronica loved the family life, it was all she ever wanted: the relationship between her and her husband was one of dependence, understanding, and commitment to each other and their family.

SOMEDAY A BLESSING

Veronica was a dedicated mother, coming from a family of thirteen. Her family was very close and often got together for family gatherings. Her parents would wake all thirteen of them up every night around midnight for snacks.

"Being so many, they must be hungry," her father said.

Veronica learned from her mother to knit and sew and she had become quite the seamstress. She made matching clothing for the girls: Sophie, Stasia, and Krystyna. Zenon, Sophie's only brother, would have matching clothes in his own little boy way. Veronica learned to be very clean and keep her children spotless, another trait she learned from her mother. There were no luxuries in Poland. In order to "bleach" their whites, they would lay their white clothes and sheets out on a sunny,

snow-covered day and would let the sun bleach them out. They called this "sun bleaching."

Veronica grew vegetables in a small garden and would milk their three goats for milk and cheese. One of Sophie's favorite chores was to take the goats alongside the country roads so they could eat the white-flowered clover found there. This was her favorite chore because this was her time to be alone and let her childish imagination take her on adventures to other places around the world. She would sit on a roadside fence or in the grass with her legs crossed while watching the goats grazing and tie endless amounts of clover stems together. She would fasten the long chains of clover stems in her hair and let the ends dangle to her feet. She felt so pretty as she walked home. Her hair decorated with fashionable jewels and long pearly necklaces wrapped around her neck—all gifts from some young prince in a faraway land. She would turn and spin and skip as her imagination soared and the three goats followed close behind her.

Frank was a small-framed man who stood tall with pride and honor. Tender was his heart toward everyone he met. He spoke with kindness of his hopes and dreams for his family. He was a coal miner and also worked part-time repairing watches. The town's people brought grandfather clocks, coo-coo clocks, and wrist watches for him to repair. Sophie remembered the many clocks that hung on their

13

walls all sounding off simultaneously throughout the night. Many patrons would have little money and Frank would often take less for his trade. His favorite hobby was to prop his leg up on a stool with his accordion on his lap and play the polka. As the music bellowed through the thin walls of their apartment, the children would gather in a circle and would dance the night away in the kitchen.

On payday every Saturday, Frank would meet with the boys from work and have a few beers before returning home. Veronica hated this vice of his and would always be waiting with a hot washtub of water and would scrub Frank to the bone trying to get the smell of beer and smoke off of him. She would scrub his face so hard seeing only the good that would come out of her anger.

He will have fewer wrinkles on him from all this scrubbing when he gets older, she would laugh to herself.

Frank knew his way home as he rode his bike from the bar after having a bit too much to drink by simply counting the number of trees he needed to pass before turning onto the street to home. One Saturday night, Frank came home a little later than usual and knocked on the door as he always did, but Veronica saw a man resembling her husband standing with a lost expression on his face, wearing an oversized hat and trench coat with the arms of the coat hanging a foot over his hands and dragging the floor.

Veronica began laughing as she said with a childlike grin, "I wonder who has your little coat." It soon became a family joke for years to come after another scrubbing in the wash tub.

Every Sunday morning, Veronica would attend early Catholic Mass while Frank would get the kids ready to go to the mid-morning assembly. While Frank and the children were at church, Veronica would be busy preparing a special Sunday dinner for her family.

The news of work in the Holland coal mines for better pay was all it took for Frank to pack his bags and board a train that week. He would work till he had enough money to buy a home, and then send for his family back in Poznan. This took almost a year. Frank stayed with other coal miners in a small apartment and saved every dime he

SOMEDAY A BLESSING

could. The letter brought excitement to the Stanski family. Sophie's
eyes lit up with the very thought of moving.

Sophie loved her father. She missed him dearly and couldn't wait
to see him again. Veronica was torn between the love for her husband
and the family she would have to leave behind in Poland when the
letter came for them to join him in Holland.

Maybe this would be the future foretold by the gypsy, Sophie
thought to herself. Her other siblings danced with enthusiasm.
Veronica welcomed this day but also dreaded it. It was to be a
permanent move, and she was not looking forward to leaving
Poznan. She desperately wanted her family back together again, so
they started to pack what they could and gave the rest of their
furnishings to Veronica's family to keep for them. In secret,
Veronica was determined to return to Poznan one day.

The train ride took them all the way through Germany into
Holland. It was a long and hard trip that took the better of two days.
The seats were made of hardwood and without any kind of cushion.
Sitting for hours was wearing on everyone. Veronica did not have
enough money for the sleeping berths that most trains offered for
such long trips. What made the trip even worse was that Stasia had
become ill the day before they boarded the train. At one point,
Veronica had asked Sophie to get under the seat and get Stasia's
medicine out of their baggage. As soon as Sophie bent down under
the seat, the train came to an abrupt stop, throwing Sophie forward,
causing her to strike her head. Crying as the goose egg grew on
Sophie's forehead, Veronica attempted to comfort Sophie. Her
attempt was disrupted by Stasia vomiting. Veronica leaned back and
sighed.

*Why did I listen to Frank, I should have just stayed home. I knew
this move was a bad omen.*

The train finally came to a halt in a small town outside of
Amsterdam. Somewhat relieved, Veronica and her four children
grabbed what they could from under their seats and ran off the train
to greet their father whom they spotted on their approach. Frank
stood there in the drenching rain holding onto the reins of a one horse

open wagon that he had borrowed from a neighbor. The children ran to him and began to search his pockets for candy like they always did when he came home from work in Poland. Veronica would make several more tedious trips back and forth from the train to the wagon with the rest of the baggage while Frank and the children continued with their happy reunion, disregarding Veronica's struggle. Veronica's mind was now made up. *This trip really was a mistake!*

As they approached a small urban neighborhood, Frank pointed out their new home. Sophie's eyes widened with delight when she saw a large two-story brick home. The yard was a lush green with red and pink tulips encircling around the many trees, lining the pathway to the front door. Across the road was a huge pond that was fed by an upper creek that emptied its crystal clear waters into the pond. They would eventually fish and skate on this pond during the winter months. As they approached the house, Frank made them all close their eyes before entering the front door. Soaked to the bone, Veronica stood with drops of rain dripping off her nose onto the baggage she clutched in both her hands and under her arms. Frank, still insisting that everyone keep their eyes closed, could be heard scuffling about the house.

"Open your eyes and come in!" Frank stood grinning from ear to ear.

The kids let out a scream of excitement running from room to room, turning on and off the electric lights.

The radiance illuminating from the chandeliers made it look like Christmas lights in every room. This was the first time they would have electric lights in their own home. Sophie couldn't believe how easily she could turn on the lights with a simple flip of a switch. The ample living room would easily accommodate the late night polka dances they loved, and, for the first time, everyone had their own bedrooms. The kitchen was one to make any lady of the house proud. Veronica had her first icebox and a dinner table that would seat the entire family comfortably. Huge windows in the kitchen let the morning sun shine in and accented the beautiful panoramic view of the Holland landscape. There were no more late night runs to the outhouse or wash tub baths in the kitchen. They now had running water and inside bathroom facilities.

Sophie quickly fell in love with Holland, the house, the country, even the wooden Dutch shoes they wore that would turn into instant ice skates when the pond would freeze over in the winter months. She loved the big snows and the evening fog rolling in over the frozen skating rink. Sophie and her siblings would set out on the pond and skate up and down the now frozen creek. The wet snow clung ever so gracefully on the spruce tree limbs. The siblings made an instant game of shaking the tree limbs so that the ice cold snow would drop onto each other's backs as they raced one another up and down the frozen trail.

The Stanski family found their new language easily learned. Frank knew enough to teach the children so they could adapt while going to their new school. Sophie often took the long way home from school, darting off into the many fields of tulips and high grasses. She would run until she found herself buried in thick lush fields of tall grass that she could hide in, her own little world. Sophie would lay for hours as she daydreamed of things to come in her new home and town.

The family could finally afford their first—fruits, bananas, apples, and pears—but the most favored of them all was this delightful thing called "chocolate." The hard candies Frank hid in his pockets in Poland soon became the lavished chocolate-covered delights.

The small neighborhood held an abundance of children. They spent hours in the streets playing kickball and running around the many windmills, creeks, and fields. Frank and the kids were happy with the move. They all made new friends, loved the schools, and the many new foods.

Veronica could not help missing her family in Poznan. Her health soon began to suffer from her depression, and she finally deteriorated to the point where she required hospitalization. Frank had no choice but to send the kids to stay with friends while he continued to work and spend his evenings at the hospital with Veronica.

While Sophie and her siblings stayed with this family, the lady of the house would make sweet rolls every morning for breakfast that had raisins in them. Sophie hated raisins because they reminded her of little bugs, and she would slyly pick them out and hide them under the plate. When the woman would wash the dishes, she would find all these little squashed raisins stuck to the bottom of the plate.

Sophie was a fanatic for cleanliness. If she spilled food on her clothing or got dirty at recess, she would go home to change and return to school. This was something that Veronica understood well about her daughter. Sophie was a neat-nick; however, her temporary adoptive family found her idiosyncrasies to be a problem and contacted Frank and told him they just could not keep Sophie anymore. They decided it was best to send her back to her father. Sophie's feelings were not the least bit hurt. In fact, she was excited at the idea of being back home with her father and soon began to take over the many duties that Veronica had once performed. She cooked, cleaned, and scrubbed the kitchen floor with the dish rag. Veronica used to get furious with Sophie when she would catch her scrubbing the floor with the same rag she had just used to wash the dishes.

Veronica was soon discharged from the hospital and returned home weak and still depressed. With a paycheck that Frank received in early 1939, there was also a written notice enclosed. It informed all workers that had arrived after a certain date that they would be laid off and would have to return to their homeland. Frank was extremely disappointed. He was making great money and did not want to leave Holland, but he had no choice due to the political upheaval that was just beginning to take place in Europe. Sophie was devastated. She had grown to love Holland so much. She had never been happier in her life, although she had not "crossed great waters" as foretold by the Gypsy. Great Waters to her was anywhere but Poland.

Upon their return to Poland, all their friends and family were there to greet them on their arrival. Frank had saved enough money

SOMEDAY A BLESSING

and was able to purchase a small grocery store with living quarters above. It was in the same neighborhood they had lived in before.

Their new home was far from the luxury they had grown accustomed to in Holland, but was made very comfortable with more money at hand. Veronica's health quickly returned and Veronica's mother, Grandma Przybl, would help in the store as well as her brothers, Stanley and Leon. Veronica was so happy to be back in Poznan. Her family came over daily and life was perfect in Veronica's eyes. Sophie and the other children as well as Frank missed their home and friends in Holland, but they were happy to have their mother back to her old self: loving, caring, and well.

Sophie was not about to forget her new language, in hope of returning one day to Holland. She could often be heard while walking the streets repeating the Dutch language out loud. She was older now, fourteen years of age, and still somewhat of a loner.

One neighbor walked over to Veronica while they were out watching the kids playing in the street. "You have a very beautiful daughter, but I think there is something wrong with her," she said, almost embarrassed to bring it up.

"What do you mean?" Veronica asked.

"Well, she is always talking to herself," the lady said looking off toward the children.

"Oh, she's not crazy, she is speaking Dutch. She doesn't want to forget the language," Veronica explained as she shook her head. Sophie's mother always spoke highly of her and covered for all of her little eccentricities.

Sophie loved staying home and helped around the house. Her older sisters, Stasia and Krystyna, would go to the park where there would be bands playing the Polka. Zenon was a big prankster, being the youngest of four and the only boy, he made his presence well-known. He was always pulling shenanigans on the girls, like when they would get all dressed up to go out, Zenon would lock them in their bedrooms and run and hide, but not before returning the skeleton key to its place above the door. Zenon would run laughing as he heard his sisters screaming at him and yelling for their mother

19

to let them out. He would stay hidden until the coast was clear. Zenon always had a joke to tell and he loved to make people laugh.

It was 1939 and the Stanski family flourished as their store business grew. Frank also continued to make more money with his clock and watch repair business on the side. The Polish government and citizens were keeping an eye on Germany. Frank often met with the men in town as they spoke of the Chancellor of Germany. Things had moved quickly since 1933 when Hitler took power as the Chancellor. He suspended many of the civil rights from the people and boycotted the Jewish businesses. They began burning books and outlawed all political parties outside the Nazi Party. Even though on January 26, 1934, Germany signed a ten-year non-aggression pact with Poland, the activities of Hitler and his Gestapo made Poland nervous as they kept Polish troops posted along the German/Poland borders. Unbeknownst to the Polish people and government was the fact that Germany and Russia had signed a covert pact that they would split up the lands of Poland between them if war was to ever break out.

The adults took heed while reading the headlines and hearing all the rumors that Europe was becoming unstable. As for fourteen-year-old Sophie, life went on as usual, paying no mind to adult talk at the dinner table or the folks gathering in their store speaking of the uncertainty of their future.

The family was off to bed early, exhausted from a busy day at the store. Sophie folded her slip to lie on her dresser, hung her dress in the wardrobe, and did a quick clean up and inspection of her room before she lay down to sleep. The store was locked and as the city lamps went out one by one, the little town of Pozan slept.

The next day, September 1, 1939, the Stanski family arose to what seemed to be a typical day in Poznan. Frank went on an errand, Veronica had gone shopping, and the children prepared to go to school. Unbeknownst to them on this day, Poland would go down in history at the hands of a madman.

Chapter Two
A War of Their Own

Orders came across the airways from the Nazi Regime with instructions to begin their attack on Poland. It was September 1, 1939, at 4:45 a.m. when the battleship *Schleswig-Holstein* launched firepower onto a Polish military complex in Westerplatte. She had been floating off the harbor by the Polish banks as a good will visit to Danzig-Neufahrwasser. The German soldiers who had been camping along the German and Polish borders began their descent into Poland after getting their signal at 4:47 a.m.

One million eight-hundred thousand German troops, along with 2,600 tanks and 2,000 air craft, became one of the fastest surprise invasions into another country in history. Polish aircraft were bombed as they sat on runways. Polish military bases closest to the German lines were surrounded by German troops and destroyed before they could awaken. The east became a military monster before the morning sun rose. By noon, the sun was darkened by fire and smoke and the smells of burning rubble and flesh ascended the nostrils of its citizens as well as its already defeated troops. With lies and deceit, the ink that the non-aggression pact with Poland and the covert pact made with Russia by Hitler was not worth the paper it was written on. Adolph Hitler had a plan, unbeknownst to most of his own military troops as well as the German citizens. Few officers knew his overall intentions, as young German soldiers sat in the fog-dampened woods awaiting their orders.

They would find themselves marching into oppositions from around the world, but not until they would have killed thousands of Poles, Jews, and destroyed millions of homes, hospitals, schools, and the cities themselves. The German troops and citizens were driven by commands, fear, or devotion to their leader. Hitler had come very close to the dreams of his evil mind to take over the world and create a perfect Aryan race.

Sophie peered out the store's window. She heard sounds similar to thunder as bottles on the shelves began to rattle. She looked up at the sky to notice there were no clouds. A flock of pigeons swooped by the window in a frenzy as feathers float calmly down in an almost airless ballet. Startled, she fell back from the window. Bewildered, she stared at the feathers as they touched the ground. She turned away from the window and laughed to herself. *How silly of me, afraid of a few feathers.*

Veronica had gone to town, and Frank was making a delivery— neither of them knowing of the fury that was about to be put upon them that day. The town's people started hearing the low-flying planes and soon visualized them, looking like huge Pterodactyls positioned like geese flying south for the winter, sweeping over the buildings. Mothers and fathers started to rush home, knowing their children had not yet left for school.

Veronica ran across the bridge over the Warta River towards home. She stopped in the middle of the bridge in terror, dropping the goods she had just purchased in town. Bomber planes were flying so low that the bridge shook beneath her and her vision blurred as tears began to well up in her eyes. Veronica's town she loved so much, the town she longed to return to from Holland, was under attack.

"My children!" She screamed, glancing over at the town square and then towards home. "Where do I go? I've got to get home! I need to find shelter!" Her mind in a panic, she stumbled over her bags and ran toward home.

SOMEDAY A BLESSING

Vendors abandoned their carts, local bands dropped their instruments in the parks, people began running frantically through the streets. The sounds of machine guns and bombs hitting the ground were all around them. The Polish government leaders were on their way out of the country, swiftly leaving in cars. They headed toward the train station, followed by the relentless shelling. All military objectives had been mapped out in red by the Reich, as Poznans population dwindled in only minutes.

It was supposed to be a beautiful, unusually warm sunny day that Friday, September 1. The fall warmth only made it harder to breathe as the dust and fumes made its way into the sultry air. Cries for help could be heard as rubble fell and crashed onto the streets. All communications were interrupted as cities, towns, and villages fell to the Nazi rule.

Staring out the store front window, Sophie and Zenon stood in astonishment as they gazed out over the streets. Filled equally with fear and excitement, Stasia was pulling at their arms to get them back upstairs to the apartment. They gathered in the kitchen. Stasia and Krystyna's eyes were fixed on each other, wondering what to do next.

Terrified, Krystyna yelled, "We don't have a cellar!"

Stasia remembered something. "The sand pile! Mom said go there and cover our faces if there was ever a chemical attack. She said if the Germans ever attacked us they won't be trying to kill us with bombs, they will probably use gas!"

They all jumped up and ran down the stairs, stopping at the main entrance to the store. Stasia nodded the approval to start running back behind the building. Kneeling into the sand pile, the four siblings reluctantly pulled their shirts over their faces. Sophie and Zenon fought every minute they had to keep their faces in the already suffocating sand. Stasia spooned the sand over the backs of their heads with her hands, getting sand in their ears and mouths. Sophie's attempts to gasp for fresh air were stifled as Stasia shoved her face back into the pile, frantically pushing the sand back over her head.

"Stop it!" Stasia yelled. "Keep your heads down!"

The ground rumbled as the plane engines roared from above. The jolts from the explosions shattered windows, and buildings began to crumble. The four kneeled helplessly, with each breath taking in particles of dust and sand into their nostrils. Too terrified to raise her head, Stasia began to pray. Her eyes closed, she whispered, "Dear Lord, I ask for your protection, over my parents, sisters, and brother Zenon. I don't know the ones who fire upon us. Please Lord, I beg of you, watch over us and bring my mother and father home safely."

At that moment, Veronica ran into the apartment. In distress, she looked about her home, and saw only the remains of a frantic scramble by her children.

"Stasia! Sophie! Where are you?" She stopped to listen as the bombings stopped in complete silence. The birds and the sounds of the city were serene.

Veronica, with tears streaming down her face, jumped as she was startled by the sound of her children flying through the door, causing it to slam it into the wall. They frantically hugged her. Veronica reached to them.

"Are you all alright?" she asked, as she searched every inch of them.

"Yes, we are, Mom. We're just fine," Stasia said, out of breath.

For a moment all seemed well as Frank ran through the door. "Get down!" he yelled.

They all fell to the floor, and started to crawl toward the pantry, closing the door behind them. In darkness, they sat through the next round of pounding explosions. It was dusk as they huddled together, not by a fireplace, nor the dinner table, but in a closet. Their faces dirty, eyes full of fear, they spent the night in their clothes, holding and leaning on one another for security.

Heads leaned on each other's shoulders; they were awakened the next morning by the faint cries of children. Rushing out of the pantry, they gazed out the kitchen window. Across the street, the Jewish family that had been their neighbors for years stood holding small bundles of clothing in their arms, forced at gunpoint by German soldiers. The Stanski family watched in horror as the family was

SOMEDAY A BLESSING

forced to join the already increasing death trail of other Jewish families. They saw lines of marching Nazi soldiers, looking like green rivers rolling down the bloodied streets of Poznan. Eyes darkened with coldness, they would split into groups of five knocking, down doors. "Raus! Get out!" They yelled. The Nazi soldiers were there to take their food, businesses, money, and anything of value in support of their Commandant, Adolph Hitler.

Thousands of Jews were marched to the makeshift death camps, and Polish soldiers sent to prisons or killed. Street signs were renamed with German names. All other languages were forbidden to be spoken or written. Nazis stormed the hospitals and mental facilities, killing all the patients, dumping their sick or crippled bodies into burned piles outside of town. Germans set up mobile gas chambers in box cars that were once used only for transport. The Germans thought it was ingenious to use the fumes from the motor exhaust itself to gas their prisoners, piped in the back of the truck as they drove to Murowana Goslina. The captives would all be dead upon their arrival and their bodies burned. The remaining ashes would then be spread out in the woods. Spruce trees were planted over the now-fertilized ground to cover up their evil deeds.

Several days had passed while Frank, Veronica, and the children sat at the dining room table, contemplating what to do next or where to go. Suddenly the door was kicked in, and five German soldiers rushed in and surrounded them. With machine guns pointed at Frank's face, the smell of gunpowder filled the room from the Germans clothing.

Feeling helpless, Frank futilely yelled out. "Take what you want!"

However, they were not there to take anything. They were there to take everything!

They shoved Frank with his family, hanging onto his clothing, crying toward the stairway. Hurriedly, they ran down the steps, followed by the sound of the soldiers' heavy boots. Leather belts clanking, guns cocked and aimed, they pushed them out the front door. Apprehensively, they stood on the sidewalk, not knowing if they were going to be taken somewhere, or maybe even shot where they stood. Time stood still as the German Nazi soldiers continued terrorizing the town around them. Several townspeople stood astutely as they were grabbed and taken away, while others would be walking around in a daze, seemingly invisible to the Germans. On this day, grace fell upon the Stanski's. They stood obscure on the walk as the soldiers passed them by.

"Frank!" a voice yelled. As he turned, he saw Veronica's brother, Stanley.

"Come with me," he motioned them toward an alleyway. They followed Stanley down the alley and through the back streets into a small apartment building where the Germans were allowing many Polish families to stay, untouched, for now. The Germans first priority was to continue their vigilante attack against the Jews.

Grandma and Grandpa Przybl sat on wooden boxes in the one bedroom apartment, as the grandchildren surrounded them. The family was together, except for Franrazek. He was Veronica's oldest brother, and was already in the Polish Army, stationed at Fort V11. News came of him being shot in the chest, and then sent to prison camp somewhere in Poland. They had no way of knowing if he was dead or alive. The adults sat around each other as they spoke softly in order for the children not to hear. Facts or rumors, they took all that they heard seriously.

Grandpa Przybl leaned back with a slight nod as he remembered when they were part of Germany and they spoke the German language.

"The king was a nice man," he reflected. His voice quivered as he continued, "Times were pretty good then."

Stanley jumped up, and with anger in his voice said, "We must stay inside and hide the kids," turning around sternly, "They are taking the Polish kids to work the fields and taking any man that can hold a gun to the front lines posing as Germans to be shot first. If you are old and feeble and found out on the streets they will just shoot you on the spot."

SOMEDAY A BLESSING

"Shush!" Veronica looked with concern toward her brother. "The kids will hear you."

Stanley sat on the floor, looking down, he lifted his head. Dismayed, he said, "There's nothing we can do, they're everywhere."

Leon walked into the room.

"Brother Leon!" Stanley stood up and asked. "Have you heard anything about Franrezek?"

"No, I have not," walking toward his mother, he kneeled and kissed her on her cheek. "I've heard nothing. I'm sorry."

Leon sat on the floor next to his mother and began to tell of his journey through the streets. "This all started because of a trick the Germans pulled. They took one of their own prisoners and dressed him in a Polish uniform, shot him, and then laid him on the radio station's lawn. Then they announced to the world that the Polish army tried to attack the radio station. They said they shot one, showing the prisoner as one of us. They wanted the British and the French to believe that we had started it all."

In disbelief, they took in every word Leon said.

"But why?" Frank asked.

Leon looked off in the distance. "They want our rivers and our industries. They hate the Jews as well as us. They talk of a perfect race. If they keep us alive, it's only to use us for work."

Veronica lowered her head and murmured, "Is it just us? Just Poland?"

"No, it isn't," Leon walked toward the door, "the Russians are coming, also."

"What?!" Everyone at the same time yelled, "The Russians?!"

Leon kneeled, "Yes, the Germans promised the Russians a part of Poland up to Bug River. People have been fleeing toward the Russian lines, only to be shot by the Red Army. All the train stations are gone. They're in Warsaw now. I don't think we can beat them. We weren't ready, and our military was not ready." As a curtain of dread silenced their breathing, Leon, with saddened heart, said, "We were never ready."

27

Stanley jumped up and stormed out the door. His mother, Grandma Przybl, followed him, begging for him to come back inside.

"I don't believe this, Mother! How could this happen? How can they just come in here and take everything we have? It's been a week now, and no one has come to help us!"

"No, that's not true," Leon said, running after him. "England and France have declared war on Germany, but for now we must do all we can to stay safe. Most importantly, we need to keep the children safe."

Frank called out to them from the hallway, hearing the warning. "There is an old barn out back, maybe the children can stay in there until we can figure out something else."

As they all walked back into the room, Veronica felt some relief that her brothers were back inside.

"We just have to stay together. No one can leave," she said.

Leon and Stanley agreed, but, being men, they could not just sit by and watch Poland being taken over by the Nazis.

Leon and Stan walked to the corner of the room as Leon told him of the underground movement in the works. "I want to join. They're calling it the Home Army, and they need our help," Leon said, his eyes scanning the room.

"Yes! We'll leave tonight while the others are asleep," Stan said with no hesitation.

"We will not be able to come back here, you know."

In dismay, Stan replied, "I know."

As night fell, the parents slipped the children out to the barn. Sophie thought how entertaining it would be, sleeping out in the barn with no adults. They could stay up all night if they wanted to. The barn was huge, with piles of loose hay. The Germans had already ransacked the place for anything of value. Up an old wooden ladder that led to a hay loft, Frank and Stan took the kids and tried to bed them down for the night. The children were so excited, however, that Frank had to scold them in order to quiet them.

"Hush now! You all have to be still, please!" Frank pleaded with them.

SOMEDAY A BLESSING

The kids were having too much fun as they threw one more round of hay at each other. Dust flew, as they coughed between giggles, but the seriousness of Frank's face indicated to them that it was time to stop playing. They lay down, pushing hay into pillows and finally settled down for the night.

Sophie was bored to tears, as she lay with her eyes catching the moon's rays through the cracks of the barn wall. She restlessly rolled her head side to side. She was tired of no school, not going to town parks. She couldn't even play out in the streets with her friends. She mumbled to herself, "I'm tired of just sitting around doing nothing, hiding out all the time, crammed up with all these people. The Germans don't want us anyway. Ah! I can't sleep!" As she tosses about, Stasia rolled over.

"Sophie, be still!"

Sophie sighed, "Oh, alright."

Morning came and the air was laced with a wintry chill. Dark clouds hung like tapestries in an art gallery over the skies, birds sang with uncertainty. The stillness was peaceful compared to all the previous events that had taken place. It was not the sound of marching feet, nor the bombs being dropped that awoke them that morning. It was the cries of the women.

"They're gone!"

Chapter Three
Keepsakes

Frank jumped up from off the bed pallet. "What is it?" he screamed.

Veronica, weakened from thoughts running through her mind, her knees buckled as she wiped the tears that had streaked her face clean. "Stan and Leon, they have left, they're gone! Oh my God, the children, Frank, go check on the children!"

Frank ran to the barn, yelling out to them. His steps frozen in time, his stomach churned as he ran through the barn door. He stopped as his eyes tried to focus through the darkened dust-filled room when a bit of hay fell from the loft. Each child slowly raised their head peeking down over the loft.

"What, Dad?"

Frank sighed with relief as he climbed up the ladder and hugged them. "Thank God you're all here."

As Frank and the children rushed back to the apartment, Veronica checked each one over.

Veronica breathlessly said, "They will not sleep out there anymore! No one will ever leave my site again."

Grandma Przybl shook her head in agreement, as Grandpa Przybl took the men over to the side.

SOMEDAY A BLESSING

"I think Stan and Leon joined the Home Army. There are many underground movements. I just wish I knew which one they went to. I guess they assumed since they have no family of their own, they should be the ones to go. We can only pray for their safety now."

It had been six months since the war started. The Germans were fighting the Russians; the Polish were fighting the Russians and the Germans. France and Britain were both fighting the Germans. All these countries had their own political views, reasons, gains, and objectives…all the while innocent blood was being shed, the blood of those who had no say, the ones who had nothing to gain. Powerless, they humbled themselves as they were marched down the endless trails of fate.

Frank had moved his family to another part of the apartment building after another family had vacated. It was getting too confined with two large families in a one bedroom apartment and the stress was becoming overwhelming. Daily, Frank would walk the streets to barter for food. He was doing some watch repairs for the Germans, but it was still less than he needed to care for his family of six.

German soldiers, who patrolled the streets, were well-fed and groomed.

Even their shoes are shined, Frank noticed as he walked past them. Walking by two soldiers leaning against the corner of a building, he overheard them talking about how amusing it was to see the people begging for food, and that they had so little money. As one tilted his head back, he smirked.

"If you don't receive what you need, you must steal it," both laughing, Frank was disheartened as he passed behind them.

Frank suddenly heard, "God, look down from heaven, what do you see? I see men, I see blood, I see blood on a dead man's hand," an old man yelled out at him, followed by a mischievous laugh.

For the first time, Frank felt inferior to the Germans' domineering ways as he began to run. Followed by the laughter from the soldiers and the old man's wailings, he found himself in his old neighborhood. He walked alongside the store that he once owned with pride. Windows were busted out, the door wide open. He

31

stepped inside the now ransacked, emptied building and saw what was once his Sunday-best clothes tossed about on the floor.

"They went through everything," he said as tears bust out like a seamless dam. He held his hands over his face. "Why God? Why? These hands are willing to work. I asked for nothing! All I ever did was care for my family, and now I can't even feed them one full meal. Now I fear for their lives every waking moment!"

Frank began to reminisce when he would hear cathedral church bells chiming; the church choir voices leisurely flowed down the village streets. Candles glowed with a yellow cast against the brass candle sticks, people kneeled in prayer as the sun made rainbows across their backs through the stained glass windows. In their Sunday-best, they funneled to their seats. Frank smiled with a glance at his four children as they sat next to one another with their hands laid perfectly upon their laps. He was so proud of his little family.

Who wouldn't be? he thought to himself.

Frank's tranquil moment was disrupted by a stranger. "Hey you! Get out of here!"

Frank's heart skipped a beat as he returned to reality. Frank knew that at that moment his life was in danger, possibly thought of as a looter. The German soldier who had just yelled at Frank motioned again for him to leave and for some unknown reason, compassionately allowed him to walk away. With one more glance back, he looked at what used to be his life.

It was April 2 and the Stanski family was holding a small birthday party for Sophie. Handmade gifts from each of her cousins and a mended dress from her mother was not like her previous birthdays. Since she had no Christmas this past year, she treasured her gifts of love and they became her new keepsakes.

Sophie was getting anxious about being cooped up all the time. All the Polish kids began to beg for some outings.

"They are not after us anymore, mother!" Sophie, with a saddened face, would say. "Can't we just take a walk? They even have the theaters open now and are playing movies that we can watch, just for us Polish."

SOMEDAY A BLESSING

Veronica was at her wit's end just struggling to survive. She finally gave in to Sophie's plea.

"You may go into town and buy us some bread!" Veronica yelled. The door slammed before she could finish her sentence.

Sophie was excited by all means as she called down the hallway to her friend Marta. "Hey, you want to walk to town with me?"

"Sure," Marta replied.

"And the theater?" Sophie continued, knowing her mother would disapprove.

"Yes!" Marta was just as excited as Sophie as they walked out the apartment door.

This was the first time Sophie got to see all the German soldiers lined up and down the streets, wearing green trench coats, rounded helmets, and machine guns strung across their shoulders. In an odd way, Sophie felt safe. The soldiers had left her father alone as he had walked the streets, and since they were protecting the city from all the other allies, Sophie assumed she and her friend would be protected as well.

Orders had come, however, from Hitler, who was well aware that the Poles would venture into town on this day. They were allowed two days a week to see movies that the Germans had hand picked for them. Germany was in dire need of workers in their factories and farms. The war had become so fierce and had grown so massive. It was taking all of Hitler's men and young boys to go to war, leaving just the women and children to work. No one was left to keep Germany's economy going.

Crossing the street, the racing motor of a German truck slammed to an abrupt stop in front of Sophie and Marta, as the tires squealed. Heavy boots hit the ground, and before the two friends could turn around, they were surrounded by German Nazis holding machine guns pointed at them. Sophie's mind shut down. In a dreamlike state, her movements slowed. Words became echoes as the men shouted out their orders

"Aufstehen! Get up!" The language barrier was broken that day by the pointed guns. Even though Sophie could not think, frozen, she

33

stared at the back of the truck and then at the street ahead of her. In the shadows of the truck bed, she saw the faces of many children huddled in lines against the walls.

"Aufstehen!" they shouted again.

Sophie thought, *Maybe they are taking us to the theater.* She thought since this was the day the Polish were allowed to see one.

Suddenly, she felt a soldier grabbing her arm as he threw her into the back of the truck. Pulling the flaps down, two soldiers climbed in the back, sitting with machine guns propped strategically on their laps. Sophie looked around at all the distraught and frightened faces. *They're all girls,* she thought.

The truck pulled off as Sophie looked through the wind-blown canvas, watching as they drove past the buildings one by one. As they passed stores and the theater, her heart sank. She knew now they were taking her away. She assumed it would be far away, just like the similar stories she'd been hearing for months. She was horrified now.

What are their intentions? she thought as she looked up at the men who sat with an adverse look about them. *What have I ever done to you?*

Dust began to fume back into the truck bed, making the children cough. It had been hours since their abduction as they made way down an old dirt road.

"Where are they taking us?" Marta whispered as the truck bumped them in and out of their sitting positions. No one answered, too scared to look, and too scared to talk. Marta put her head down, and spoke no more.

Stopping violently, the truck came to a halt. The canvas was thrown up over the top; hurriedly a German soldier ordered them to get out. This time it was spoken in Polish. They were in front of some old wooden slat building with flat roofs and dirt floors and they were forced to go inside. Sophie saw only young girls, all between the ages 14 and 16, it appeared. Sitting on the floor, Sophie tried to close her eyes but could not keep her mind from racing with thoughts about what was going to happen to them.

Are they taking us to death camps? Or maybe even use them to work in the factories? she wondered to herself.

"I wish I had paid more attention to the stories my folks spoke about. Then maybe I might know what could happen to us," Sophie said quietly to Marta.

One of the girls leaned over toward Marta.

"They want us as sex slaves for the German soldiers," she said.

"I don't believe that!" Marta replied.

"But we're all girls, what else would they want us for?" the girl answered as she leaned back shrewdly.

Sophie curled up on the dirt floor. Hearing the talk she could not stop the tears that welled up in her eyes. Her body shook as she fought to keep from vomiting. She was afraid the soldiers might kill her for making a mess if that happened.

Why did I have to go to town? Why? My mother knew it was too dangerous, she knew, and she was right. Why didn't I listen to her? Sophie scolded herself.

As visions of her parents' faces flashed before her eyes, she tried to burn their images into her brain. *I will never forget what they look like, never.*

Sleep came late for some. Before the sun rose, they would be awakened. Sophie looked around the room, seeing that they had brought more girls in through the night. Coerced out the door, they escorted all of the girls around to the back and told them to strip down as soldiers stood nearby holding the ends of water hoses. The young victims stood huddled together covering their nakedness with their hands as the soldiers began spraying them with cold freezing water. The girls stood, crying, screaming, and gathered into circles to keep each other warm. Another hose came out from behind the crowd of soldiers, pointing at them. The girls turned their backs and cried out.

"No, God. No!" Thinking it could be a poisonous spray, white powder spewed out covering them like a blanket of snow. It was delousing powder. Sophie let out a sigh of relief. Spraying them again with the cold water, they were then told to put their clothes back on. Sophie knew at this point they were probably not going to kill them but send them into the German workforce.

"I will not work for them, no way! I'd rather die first!" Marta said to Sophie.

Sophie replied, "Me, neither. I'm going home."

Dressed, they were put back on the truck for a short distance that came up on a train station. Box cars were already filled to the brim with Poles, Jews, and prisoners of war sitting on the railway tracks.

Sophie again became doubtful of their intentions. *Maybe I'm wrong. Maybe they are sending us to the death camps,* she thought.

With wooden steps placed in front of the box car doors, the girls were forced to line up as soldiers prodded them into the cars. As Sophie stepped in, she was shoved toward the back of the straw-covered box car. There were buckets placed in the corners for toilets. The huge door squeaked along the metal tracks, slamming shut, iron against iron, as the large hook crossed over into the looped brackets. The soldier hit the lock, securing his cargo, and walked away.

Darkness set in as Sophie attempted to focus on the small cut out windows. Sunlit dust floated onto her face as she frantically squirmed herself toward them. Cut fencing nailed across them, Sophie started to pound and attempted to push the fencing out.

"Let me out! Let me out of here!" she yelled.

"Stop it. You're going to get us in trouble!" The other girls said while they tried to pull her away from the window.

"I'm jumping out!" Sophie screamed.

Marta took her arm and pulled harshly, "You can't get through there, so stop it! We're going to get in trouble! They might kill us all." Marta pleaded to Sophie.

Sad and intimidated, she peered out a small crack as tears streamed down her already swollen face. "Father! Mother! I'm here! Come get me, please! I'm here, right here!" she cried out one more time as she crumpled to her knees on the hay and sobbed.

The locomotive steam blew as the train began to pull forward while each box car was jolted into a forward motion, throwing the unwilling passengers into each other. Startled, they let out screams and cries, as the iron wheels slowly crept down the tracks. Many fearful, teary faces struggled to see out the cracks and windows, seeing only an endless assembly of the SS and the Nazi soldiers.

As night fell, Sophie felt a pain in her stomach, having not eaten in two days. She was cold and dirty. She curled up against Marta, falling into a restless sleep.

For two more days they remained in the box car, stopping in unrecognizable towns. Sophie had no idea what country she was even in. The girls were getting weaker as an eerie silence filled the car. Only whimpers and muffled coughs could be heard.

Awakened by the sounds of steel brakes squealing, the train halted. The doors were unlocked and forcefully pushed open. Incoherent, the girls were still laying down. They arose, squinting into the sunlight.

"Get up! Out! Out!" the Nazis yelled, as they pulled them out by their legs and feet.

"Shit, they stink!"

"Dirty Pollock's! Line up! Over there! You stupid Poles!"

"This one's dead!" a soldier yelled. "What do I do with her?"

"Throw her in the coal train," another soldier replied.

Sophie could not understand what they were saying, but by the looks on their faces, she knew it was a look of disgust toward them. Later, she would find out they were thought of as treasonists against their own country. They should have killed themselves before being captured by the Germans. The open box cars that were used to haul coal were now where they put the dead bodies of people who had died on the trains.

Standing in roll-call-type squares, Sophie looked over and saw another group, all boys, all about the same ages as themselves. Her eyes met up with a young boy, no words spoken. They stared at each other, knowing they had the same questions and neither had an answer. Her head lowered when she sensed a welcomed odor as the wind blew casually by. Her stomach started to churn, feeling like air bubbles bellowing up in her throat.

Food! she thought, *For us? Oh, God, please let it be for us!*

"Move it!" The soldiers yelled as they surrounded them, pushing them toward some tables with large steel pots sitting on them. Loaves of bread lay on the bare table tops. Famished, the children started running toward the food, only to be hit by the butts of the German guns.

"Halt!" they commanded as they came out of nowhere, encircling them. Guns pointed, the children stopped, lowering their heads for fear of being shot.

Suddenly, a boy spoke out with anger in his voice. "Please, we are hungry! We just want something to eat!" Sophie just knew they were going to shoot him.

The boy lowered his head and spoke in a softer tone, "We just want to eat."

The soldiers drew their guns back and stepped aside. Humbled, the children formed into a line, each one licking their lips with anticipation looking over each other's shoulders, hoping there would be enough for all of them.

Small tin cups were filled from a dipper full of potato soup and a slice of bread cut off by a stocky SS lady. The children scarfed it down without even noticing that it had potato skins in it. Sophie noticed, however, she was too hungry to pay it any mind on this day. Looking around, they began stuffing some of the bread into their pockets and clothing, not knowing if this was going to be their last meal.

Only minutes passed as the soldiers started yelling at them. "Up!"

The weather changed quickly as dark clouds rolled in, sprinkling drops of rain. The children raised their heads up to the sky, opening their mouths. They welcomed any small droplets on their tongues and washed their hands and faces. Soldiers motioned them to line up and pointed them toward a road. Up the hill made of red clay, the road quickly became slippery from the now pouring down rain. They could not see what was up over the top, but the hill became treacherous as each step was caked in red mud. Some were already physically exhausted, cold, wet, and undernourish. Some were

SOMEDAY A BLESSING

sickened with disease and collapsed, only to be beaten by the SS men with the butts of their guns.

One boy, struggling to walk along side Sophie, slipped and fell into the muddy trail and now refused to continue. Sophie glanced down at him and inconspicuously made a motion with her head attempting to encourage him to follow while she continued to struggle to make the hill herself. As she walked, she heard the sound of gunfire and was too frightened to turn around. In her heart, she knew it was probably the boy being shot. Sophie reached for all the inner strength she could muster and in a running walk, she reached the top. Sophie would learn quickly that the SS, upon their discretion, could make their own codes of conduct. Any way they felt fit, they could punish a prisoner.

Sophie was out of breath and saw before her a beautiful mountain range in the distance while the lightening from the thunderstorms illuminated the skyline. The other children quickly reached the top of the hill. Sophie heard a gasp from the crowd and turned to her left to where she saw watchtowers at the four corners of what appeared to be some sort of a prison camp. The camp was surrounded by 15-foot fencing with brackets elbowed over toward the inside of the camp holding strands of barbed wire to prevent any escapes.

It was the concentration camp, Dachua, outside of Munich, Germany. This camp was built in 1933 by the Germans and had primarily been used for criminals and political prisoners. Across the gate read the words, "Arbeit Macht Frei" (Work Makes Free). The camp was well-known for its torture and starvation tactics, although they did not have mass killings there. Most of the prisoners died from the elements, disease, or were simply worked to death. The prisoners' heads were shaved and they were forced to wear striped fatigues as another way to dishonor them. During the war, the camp was used as a holding place for workers. Any private firms in Germany were able to come and take their pick of the detainees for free labor. Taking them by day and returning them at night, most worked in the Armament factories. Soon there would be more to choose from with all the prisoners of war and the kidnaping of the 1,000 children off the streets of Poznan.

Chapter Four
Work Makes Free

Through the back gates, they walked into what was surprisingly a barren prison with no prisoners in site, only a few soldiers standing guard. The yards around the barracks were raked all to perfection, no trash—everything was spotless. Sophie thought it was kind of strange that a prison was kept so tidy, a far cry from what she had imagined a prison to look like.

The sun breaking through the clouds brought much-needed warmth to the children as they sat down, warming themselves and hoping the sunshine would help them to dry off. The smell similar to wet dogs set in as the sun broke out and the humidity rose. Although it looked clean, the odor of the unsanitary conditions soon became obvious. Sophie held her nose as the SS men separated the boys and girls and sent them into barracks. There were bunk beds in levels of three with striped- cloth feathered mattresses on the plywood box springs, flattened with what few feathers were left, if any. No pillows…only a small brown, moth-eaten wool blanket.

The girls picked out their bunks and laid flat on their backs.

"Ah, it feels so good to stretch out," Marta said as she leaned over the bunk. "Sophie, how are you doing?"

"Oh me? I'm fine, I guess. I just wish I was home. I just can't believe I'm here and this is happening to us," Sophie replied.

"Don't we all," one girl said. "I think we're here to work in the factories and the boys will go to the front lines."

"Front lines?" a couple of girls say in unison.

"Yes. They dress them up as German soldiers and make them walk in the front of the real German soldiers so they get shot first."

"That's terrible," one girl answered.

Another asked, "What about the factories? I've heard they're really bad, too. They work you until you can't work any more and then kill you."

"When you can't work anymore?" one asked.

"Oh yes, you don't get near the food or the rest that you need, and then they beat you and maybe rape the girls."

"Then what would be the best place?" Another asked.

"If you had to choose, no where. It's all bad, we're better off dead, I think," another girl responded.

"Stop it! Stop talking like that. You are scaring everyone!" Marta blared out.

"I don't care. It's true." The girl took a deep breath and said, "Well, that's what I've heard anyway."

"See there," Marta said. "She doesn't even know for sure. It's just what she's heard…it means nothing."

"Then why are we here?" a young girl asked.

Sophie raised her head in her direction, hoping someone would give an answer she wanted to hear.

The room silenced. Nobody answered as everyone lied back on their beds.

"Marta?" Sophie whispered.

"Yes, Sophie?"

"Don't leave me, ever. You promise?"

"I'll do my best, Sophie. I promise."

Early the next morning Sophie and Marta heard several girls yelling out.

"Come here, Come here," as they saw a girl motioning to the others to come to the window.

"Prisoners! Look at all of them."

"How do they look?" one asks.

"They're all men."

"Let me see, let me see," the girls pushed their way up to the doorway.

The excitement of seeing other people, as they might know someone, quickly changed to a feeling of dread as men with daunted faces and dirty clothes walked by, dragging their feet. They held their heads low, beaten, and soulless. The boys were out in the prison yard, sitting around as the guards kept watch between them and the girls' barracks. They all watched in horror as the skeleton figures in striped fatigues marched between the fence and a muddy water-filled canal.

One of the boys insubordinately walked toward the fence. He reached into his pocket, crumpled a piece of his bread and threw it over the fence. At first, no one noticed the life-giving bread that fell on the path until one old famished man leaned down and picked it up. Looking around to make sure a SS was not watching, he shoved it in his mouth. The other children witnessed this one boy's courage and compassion toward another human being. All the children ran to the fence and also began to throw their bread rations to the prisoners. The situation soon became out of control and frenzied as the prisoners ran up to the fence begging for more. Some of the bread fell into the canal and quickly became soggy, but it did not stop the men, as they continued to jump into the water, dishing up the food in the palms of their hands, consuming what pieces clung to their wet fingers.

Sophie thought they looked like striped fish jumping in and out of the water and as it became muddy, it still did not slow them down.

The SS men feared a riot and started jumping into the water. They jabbed the men with their bayonets.

"Halt!" they yelled, but hunger overpowered the prisoners and with the children's mercy for them, the frenzy continued. Soldiers once again encircled them, with guns pointed. The prisoners on their knees began to weep as the children were made to return to the barracks. When they glanced back, they saw them pulling out bodies from the canal. Sophie wondered if they should have even thrown them the bread. Now some are dead because of what they thought was a good deed.

"Seems you can't do anything right in here," Marta said.

"I can't do anything right." Sophie laid her head down, her mind racing back and forth to her family and then to the event that had just occurred. *I wish I'd never gone to town that day, and now what do I do? I wonder what mother is thinking. She probably thinks I'm dead. I wish I could tell you, Mother, that I'm here. I'm alive! I wish you could come get me.*

The next morning they brought the children in front of tables, clipboards and ink pens laid out meticulously in front of the stoic SS personnel. No food was provided for the children because of the ruckus they had caused the previous day with the prisoners. SS asked for their names and nationality. Sophie was given a black arm band with a large letter "P" sewn in white and was told to wear it at all times or else she would be shot.

Led to the train once again, the girls were being separated. SS women came in between Marta and Sophie. Sophie grabbed Marta's hand.

"No! No!" Sophie screamed.

The soldiers forced their way between them and struck Marta on the shoulder with the butt of their guns. The two still did not let go.

"No! My God, please help us!" Sophie again yelled.

The SS threw Marta to the ground; Sophie was drug, still hanging onto Marta's hand. The SS again started stomping on their arms.

"No! I can't live without you, Marta!" Sophie cried.

Their hands were being pulled apart and then one final stomp by a SS woman on their arms forced them to let go. Sophie was then thrown into the box car, as Marta was drug away to an unknown destination. They both fought for their lives on that day. The only hope they had to make it through another day was broken by the German SS will.

Marta was never heard from again. Her family back in Poznan never had her body returned to them, nor received any knowledge of where her remains were. She gave her life for one man's dream of taking over the world in one day. She never received any recognition for losing her life. Marta died fighting for no just cause. She was only a little girl and had made the mistake of taking a walk through streets of her hometown on that fateful day.

Sophie, not knowing of the outcome of her friend, had decided she was going to take her own life by starving herself to death. They weren't feeding her much anyway, so she had become accustomed to the hunger pangs already. It sounded like the best idea. Sophie knew she would be on the train for days, so maybe she would be dead when they opened the door and it would all be over. She figured her family might be dead also, so what difference would it make? Not hearing any good news about the war, Sophie knew her family could not escape to other countries, but maybe they had gotten out. Maybe they packed up and left, thinking she was never coming back. Sophie didn't know what to believe at this point.

Sophie was in the right frame of mind. She would complete her plan to commit suicide by starvation. To her surprise, the train, after only a few hours, came to a stop. The doors flung open, and she was in front of a large white building. It looked like some sort of school house. There were very few SS men as they motioned her to go in the front door of the building. She looked around and saw a line of chairs sitting in a half circle with civilians standing around the corner. Guards stood by each doorway as the SS escorted the children seating them one by one down the row of chairs. As male civilians scanned the room, they would whisper to one gentleman, who would in turn point a finger at you, curling it back up motioning for you to come his way.

A little man appearing to be in his thirties looked at Sophie and told the officer he wanted her. Sophie found out soon after that his wife had just had twins and needed help with the house work, but Sophie had already made up her mind. She was not going to work for the Germans. Motioned to follow him outside, he grabbed his bike and pushed it while Sophie followed. She briefly thought of running, but she had no idea where she was and SS were stationed on each

45

street corner, holding large intimidating German Shepard dogs on a leash. She would just stick to her original plans.

Coming up on a quaint little home, the lady of the house came out on the porch to great them. With a seemingly friendly smile, she motioned for them to come inside. She had three-week-old twin girls and desperately needed help with them. She had no idea that Sophie was firm on the decision she had made earlier that day. Visions of Marta and herself being pulled apart and the SS stomping on their arms to separate them had Sophie in a mind set.

They showed her the kitchen, and tried to instruct her to do the dishes and scrub the floor. Weakened by her already self-destructing starvation, she walked to the corner of the kitchen and curled up on the floor. They tried to get her up and offered her some food but Sophie just laid there sobbing. The German couple appeared to be kind people and maybe even felt sorry for her. They welcomed free help, but only from a willing and compliant worker. They wanted nothing to do with mistreating their help. Sophie fell asleep on the floor, and the couple left her there for the night.

"Maybe she will come around tomorrow," the woman said to her husband.

The next morning, Sophie remained on the floor and the German couple felt that maybe she was sick and feared she may infect the babies with something. They took her to a doctor that morning. Checking her over thoroughly, the only thing the doctor could conclude was, "Home sick, that's all," the doctor said.

Feeling helpless, the couple took her back to the house and decided to send her back to the placement building. As she sat in the same half circle, she felt that surely they would send her home this time. If they could not make her work, Sophie thought she had won the game. In hopes of going home, a SS woman stood in front of her speaking broken Polish.

She said, "You are not going home, so give it up. You will work!"

Sophie sat in fear. She felt the German family would not have hurt her, but if she came back here again the SS would kill her next time. Taking her own life she could deal with, but being tortured by the

Germans scared her into wanting to live again. She began thinking about returning home and thinking that maybe her family was there waiting for her and how her mother would react to the news of her death. She decided to do what the Germans asked of her.

This time an SS woman motioned for her to follow her. Walking a short distance, they came to a bus. They stepped inside and sat down next to each other. Sophie had no idea where they were taking her this time.

Maybe a factory? she wondered, frightened at the thought of being sent to one. She prayed for another place. *Please, God, don't let them send me there. I'll be good and do what they tell me, please.*

They drove down a well-maintained paved road. Over on the left, it looked like a power plant. A large river ran through an outlook tower positioned on a dam and on through a grove of trees. On the right side was a very well-kept farmhouse set up on a slight incline. Steps were cut out of the hillside up to the front porch. The lawn was landscaped down the slope toward a black iron fence along a road sculpted in fancy laid stones. The front porch was red brick with several cast iron tables and chairs. The house was of stucco exterior with brown, painted wood trim. Off to the side was a huge two-story barn made out of the same matching material as the house. Fields in crop and hay lay green and lush lined by perfectly straight and narrow fence lines.

The bus stopped in front and Sophie could not believe this was the place. *It's beautiful,* she thought. Thinking maybe all she had to do was clean house and work in the kitchen, she thought, *I can do this easily enough.*

It was a wonderful looking place. Her spirits rose as she walked up the steps following behind the SS woman. Greeting her at the door was a nice looking German lady who, with a smile, spoke to her kindly.

"Hello, my name is Adelaide. Come in." Sophie had picked up a little German language and had been warned about speaking any Polish after the takeover of Poznan. She listened contently to what was being said and kept quiet as the lady of the house took her back toward the kitchen, Adelaide waved the SS woman off. It was as if she were saying "It's alright, she'll be fine." Sophie felt a feeling of peace and acceptance as she looked around. For some strange reason, it felt like a home. Adelaide touched her shoulder gently and pointed to some shoes on the back porch. Adelaide gave her some oil and rags, making a scrubbing motion. She handed Sophie the first pair. Sophie got on her knees and began to clean the shoes as Adelaide patted her again on her shoulder. By the time she was done, Adelaide called out to her.

"Come get something to eat."

Sophie had smelled the food warming up and hoped she could satisfy her hunger that had come back ten-fold. After her meal, thinking she needed to clean up, three little girls bounced into the kitchen through the back door. All three looking younger than eight, and she smiled as they passed her, heading toward the cookies. Adelaide motioned to her to come out on the porch and handed her some sheets and one feather down blanket. In the corner were some steps that went up to a small room, wood slabs were the walls, one window, a night stand and a twin bed was all that decorated the room. Adelaide motioned her to make her bed, and went back down stairs.

While Sophie was making her bed, male voices echoed upstairs and Sophie strained to hear and understand what they were saying. It sounded like an argument, but she was so overwhelmed with lack of sleep, she lay on the bed and quickly dozed off.

Well before dawn, she heard a man's voice yell up at her from her bedroom window. She wearily rose and stood by the window looking down. She saw a man wearing a plaid shirt, light brown pants with knee-high rubber boots. Motioning with his hands for her to come outside, Sophie slowly stepped down the stairs one by one, looking and listening for someone to greet her at the bottom. When Adelaide burst from around the corner holding rubber boots, she startled Sophie, causing her to jump. Adelaide smiled, handed her the boots, and pointed her out the back door. Adelaide's husband stood in the dark, and pointed to himself.

"Alun. My name is Alun," he said. Sophie nodded as they walked toward the barn. Yawning, she stood in a sparsely-lit barn as Alun slid open a door letting in two Holstein milk cows. The cows walked right toward a feed bin, placing their heads inside wooden slats that slid against their necks and under a carved wooden hook that locked their heads in place. Only their bodies could move from side to side. Placing a stool by one cow's udders, he called to her. "Come here, sit," he said.

Sophie had watched her mother milk goats before, but she had never tried it herself and the size of the cow was very intimidating as she looked at its legs that were bigger around then her own. Alun told her again to sit on the stool. As she approached slowly, she sat down. Alun handed her a bucket pointing his finger, "Milk."

Sophie thought, *Surely he does not think I know how to do this.*

Alun walked over to another cow and started to milk. Sophie was stunned and sat looking around hoping he would get disgusted with her and send her back in the house.

"I can do housework," she said, thinking aloud.

Alun slammed his bucket down and walked toward Sophie with a look between frustration and anger on his face. Sophie hurriedly grabbed a tit, holding her head down low, and started to squeeze it.

"No, no," he said with a stern voice.

He grabbed her hands and placed them on the cow's tits, forcing her thumb and index finger around them and then sliding it down.

"There. Milk these two, than these two."

Sophie took a deep breath. It would take 30 minutes to milk the one cow. Alun milked four other cows in the time Sophie milked one.

Shaking his head in doubt he said, "We will be back at four."

Sophie nodded, not knowing a word he had just said and thought shrugging her shoulders, *Maybe he thinks I did a good job for the first time.*

Back at the house, after straining every muscle in her thin arms carrying two large buckets of milk, Adelaide and Alun began to demonstrate to Sophie how to strain the milk and pour it into milk cans. A two-wheel cart sat outside the back door, and Alun asked her to carry one of the milk cans as he carried the other and put it up on the cart. Pointing her toward a small dirt path along side the yard, he indicated to her to push the cart down to the road. Fighting to keep her balance, she made it to the road and before she could set her end down, a German army truck pulled up and soldiers jump out. Sophie froze, thinking they were going to kidnap her again. Instead, they grabbed the full milk cans, replacing them with empty ones. She soon learned this was her early morning chore after milking. The farmers had to contribute much food to the German forces to keep them strong for fighting this evil war.

Breakfast was ready when she got back in the house: sausage, pancakes, and eggs. It was a feast to her. She was left alone to eat in the kitchen while the family sat in the dining room. Sophie started looking around the kitchen, and thought how huge it was.

Why would you want two ovens and four sinks? she thought to herself. Her back to the porch door, she heard the door slam shut. Looking out of the corner of her eye, she saw an old man standing behind her, staring her down. Sophie looked up and around at him, and gave a small one-sided smile as he bolted around toward the dining room swinging doors muttering to himself.

Sophie was in a daze. *Hmm...wonder who that is?*

Again, she heard an argument break out in the dining room.

I wish I could understand what was being said. She somehow knew it was about her. Later, she would learn that they all wanted her to do their work. Alun wanted her to do all the milking, Adelaide wanted her to help with the kids and restaurant that opened on Sundays and the old man, who was Alun's father Vernon, wanted her to work the fields.

Sophie ended up doing nearly everything on the farm in the end. Within weeks she learned how to milk the cows, but during this time her wrist would become so sore and stiff that they would swell and ache every night. Alun would simply bound them up tightly with cloth and send her back out to the barn to continue milking, everyday, twice a day. Soon, she made the trip to the barn for milking on her

SOMEDAY A BLESSING

own. She passed the time by squirting milk in the barn cats' faces and daydreaming that someday her prince would come and rescue her.

In the winter time she really hated getting up, especially in the unheated room. She was forced to climb out of the blankets where she had created a bubble of warmth. Every morning rain, sleet, hail or snow, Alun or Vernon would yell up through her bedroom window to awaken her to yet another day of endless thankless chores. The barn was as drafty as the winter winds howled through the cracks. Sophie would bury her face into the flanks of the cows to warm her nose.

Four months had passed and Sophie had learned to speak German fluently, with no more misunderstandings from then on. Saturdays she spent in the kitchen, preparing cakes and pies from scratch, up to 60 in one day. She washed all the dishes, pots, and pans. She was not allowed in the dining room, but placed the servings on the plates as Adelaide served them to the customers. Sometimes Sophie would peer out the swinging doors catching a glimpse of all the families sitting around the tables, talking and laughing, sometimes hugging one another. Sighing and holding back the tears, she would see the burned images of her mother and father back in her mind.

God, I miss them. I wish I could tell them I was alive, and then maybe they could come and get me.

Adelaide hit the door with her foot, knocking it into Sophie's head. "Well, Sophie, what are you doing so close to the door?" she asked.

Sophie stood back and began to cry, not from getting hurt, but to cover up her thoughts of home. Knowing all along that she had been watching the families on Sunday through the doors, Adelaide looked at her with concern.

"Maybe you could write a letter to your family."

Sophie lit up and wiped the tears from her eyes.

"Please?" she pleaded.

"I think we can," Adelaide smiled.

Sophie cleaned the kitchen and finished the dishes in record time and began looking for a pen and paper.

Adelaide instructed Sophie, "The SS will have to read what you write before you can send the letter, so say nothing about where you are or with whom. Say nothing of what has happened to you. Say only that you are alright. Do you understand?"

Sophie nodded yes, agreeing to anything Adelaide asked if it would grant her the chance to write her family. It was the hardest letter she ever wrote, so much to say and ask.

July 9, 1940
Dear Mother,
    I send you blessing. I'm alive, and doing well. I'm not in a camp, or factory. I miss you all so much. Is everyone there with you? I want to come home. I wish you could come get me. I love and miss you all so much. Please write me back at the address on the envelope. They won't let me tell you where I'm at.
    Love and kisses, I love you all,
    Sophie Stanski

The letter was shortened by the SS to just, "I'm alive, and doing well, write back to address on envelope, love and kisses." She received a letter a month later from her mother that stated for her to be a good girl and do what they say, they were all alive and well. "Take care, love you so very much." All else was blacked out, but it made Sophie feel much better knowing they were still in Poznan and still living. Sophie did her duties well, even though she hated to wake up so early in the morning. After she had laid awake most of the night thinking of all that has happened to her so far, she was glad to be alive and now more than ever since she heard from her mother.

In the mornings, she heard the voice of Vernon, the grandfather, yelling up at her. His voice made her cringe. She hated to work for him because he never really needed the help; he just wanted to intimidate her. He would always find a reason to call her a dumb Pollock. Once Vernon had Sophie lead the work horses to maintain a straight line while he plowed. Sophie, however, lost her

SOMEDAY A BLESSING

concentration when she heard the train across the field, the train she saw daily. But on this day, Sophie allowed her mind to wander too much and she inadvertently allowed the horses to drift off the chosen path toward the tender green alfalfa.

"You stupid Pollock! Look what you've done! You let the horses step all over the alfalfa!"

Sophie looked down and sure enough the work horses were in heaven eating the tender grasses. She let out a scream knowing he was going to come after her and away she went running toward the house. Vernon took off after her waving a sickle around and around his head as he high-stepped with heavy rubber knee-high boots trying to catch Sophie. She wore boots, also, but they did not stop her from out running the old man to the house yelling for Alun.

The very next day Vernon yelled up at her bedroom window. "Sophie! Come out now."

She could not believe it. It was him again. Carefully, she followed him out to the barn as he stood by a grindstone. Wet-wheels were used to sharpen hatchets and blades. The wheel was made out of a large tire-shaped stone and someone had to turn the wheel with a handle making the stone circle run through a trough of water. Water was needed to keep the stone wet. Sophie's job was to turn the stone and keep the trough full of water. She turned looking off in the distance and, as always, she began daydreaming. It was the only way she could keep from going insane.

"Faster! Faster!" Vernon yelled, knowing she was not paying attention to him. She started to turn the wheel, dipping water into the pail with the other hand. Vernon stood in front of the wheel, legs spread. She noticed that water was spraying up on his crotch, as she looked again. The faster she went the more it spattered, so faster and faster she went. When the job was done as she looked at his crotch and started to laugh. Vernon screamed out to her.

"You stupid Pollock. I'm going to kill you!" Off they went again, Sophie running way ahead to Alun for safety.

Vernon would also make Sophie help him rid the barn of the many huge ugly rats that had made their home in the feed room. Vernon

53

would shuffle through the feed room scaring the rats through a hole. Sophie's job was to catch the rats in a gunny sack as they tried to escape, only finding themselves being trapped in a sack. Once Vernon felt the bag was full enough of rats, he would come outside and grab the sack from Sophie. Vernon would twist the sack opening tightly closed. Grabbing with both hands, Vernon would start smashing the bag against the barn wall. He appeared to enjoy not only killing the rodents but seeing the horror on Sophie's face as she watched the gunny sack become saturated with the blood while the rats met their doom. Sophie felt this was just another way Vernon tried to intimidate her into working freely for him. Just by the look on his face while he murdered the rats made her feel that he could do the same to her and never blink an eye.

Soon Sophie and Vernon had an unspoken understanding. If Vernon was to keep Sophie working for him and not running off to Alun, he was going to have to stop being so irritated by her constant pay backs. Even though Sophie never really stopped trying to irritate him, Vernon would shake his head but say nothing. Sophie never stopped trying to aggravate him and when she was supposed to throw a pitchfork of hay to the wagon below, she would wait for him to walk by and deliberately threw it onto his head.

Summer of 1944, Sophie continued to work, doing everything but the plumbing. She was 18 now: her teenage years gone. She wore the same two outfits' everyday with knee high boots. They lacked in every way she was used to dressing. Her monthly menstrual cycles would bring her to the rag barrel on the back porch. She would have to fold the rags up and use them for pads in her worn underwear. Embarrassed, Sophie would hide the bloody rags in crevices around the house or barn. Vernon would always find them and parade them around in front of her on the end of a stick.

She ate alone in the kitchen with no family to carry on conversations, no school, overnights, or holiday celebrations. The three little girls would show off around her wearing their pretty clothes, mocking her work actions, sneering at her. They knew she could do nothing to defend herself. The only time she ever got off the farm was to go to town on errands for the German family, and that was far and few between. Sophie passed her days in a fantasy world, looking off to the passing trains that she felt sure it held her knight in shining armor, being the princess of the fortress that held her captive. Her long gown draped her fair skin legs. Long, golden hair curled naturally over her shoulders as she awaited her rescue.

It was a hot summer, she and Vernon made their way out to the fields, all she could think about was going for a cool swim. The river across the road held an abundance of fish and cool waters rushing from the power plant. She stood frowning at the request of Vernon to help spread the cow manure on the fields from the two-wheel wagon. She dumped her shovels full next to the wagon, instead of slinging it around as instructed. With each dump, Vernon's face got redder and redder. He couldn't take it anymore: he had it with her. Soon the race was on. Sophie ran up along the fence line that ran along the road, holding on to her shovel for protection if he caught her. People were walking on the road and yelled at her to, "Run, little girl, run!" She ran like a deer, she would say, and he never did catch her. She often wondered what he would have done had he caught her on that day. The actions of the day left her alone, since the rest of the family had gone to town. Vernon had gotten overheated from his own anger and trying to run after her and sat in the living room until he passed out from exhaustion. Sophie took advantage of the situation and went swimming.

She never did learn to swim well, never venturing out far from the banks. She remembered an old pond in Poznan where the kids would go and play in the water. The owner hated these kids and would always watch out for them and run them off. One day, Sophie and her siblings along with several other friends went to the pond. Not long after, they heard the farmer yelling and saw him running toward them. All the others scattered like wild cats leaving Sophie in a panic in the pond. The more she paddled the farther out in the pond she went. The farmer grabbed her up out of the water and took her home. She remembered how scared she was, more from the near drowning than the farmer chastising her.

With this in mind, she was very careful as she stepped on the river rocks. The warm day had brought out many folk fishing and swimming. She went further down the river, this time, to be alone. Not knowing of the undercurrents, she immediately started floating off toward the middle of the river, and again with each stoke she went further out. Sophie could not believe it. As she struggled to get her footing, she kept sliding on the slippery, moss-covered stones. As the rapids grew fiercer the further she drifted, she started taking in water. Coughing and trying to catch her breath after each wave overcame her, she was going under. Exhausted, she sank to the bottom being thrashed about by the currents onto the rocks. Suddenly, a light appeared far off in the distance in the murky waters. She had never opened her eyes before under water and she thought to herself, *Is this what it looks like under here? How beautiful it is! It's so bright!*

As she felt herself being pulled closer to a large rock despite all her fighting, and she heard an encouraging voice.

"Sit. Don't be afraid…you're going to be alright."

The river current rammed her into the rock. She looked up and saw an old gray-haired, bearded man standing on the rock. Gazing at her with a surreal glow that surrounded him, she felt so calm she let go of her last breath.

Pain suddenly hit her shoulder as she was yanked out of the water. She gasped for a breath of air, thrashing her arms about.

As she was being pulled from the water a stranger was telling her, "Stop fighting me, I'm only here to help you."

She looked at his face and wondered where the gray-haired man she had just seen seconds before while she was drifting in and out of consciousness. The fisherman laid her on the bank. Soon others rushed over as one of them said, "I know who she is. She works up on the hill."

They carried her to the farm house where they put her to bed and sent for the doctor. She was to stay in bed for three days and the doctor said she would be fine. Later, she heard her ordeal was in the newspaper, a story about the fisherman saving her out of the raging river.

Sophie enjoyed her three days off, and daydreamed her time away, thinking of the old man that told her to sit.

Sit, she thought, *How strange, in the water?*

There never really was an old man, but a voice that told her to sit while she was being pulled toward him by the currents and by her not fighting, she floated freely to him. She never ventured any farther than ankle high in the river after that, splashing her face was just fine.

She loved the farm life, the riches, and the friends she had made that came to see her. Entertaining them in the large sitting area, the plush high back chairs angled toward a crackling fire, brandy glasses clanked between laughter.

"Sophie! Get to sweeping, the customers will be here soon," Adelaide said while with a sweeping motion about her arms. Sophie came out of her daydream in a daze, sometimes not even knowing where she was or what she had been doing.

How long will I be here? She thought to herself as tears welled up in her eyes. She finished sweeping the porch and steps, and returned to the kitchen to help dishing up the foods.

Out in the pasture rounding up the milk cows for their milking, Vernon and Sophie turned in shock, as a huge low flying plane roared over the power plant heading right for them. She had not heard directly who was coming, but listening to the small talk through the kitchen doors there were allied forces landing on German territory. Vernon could see that it was not a fighter plane as papers began to fly out the sides of the plane. Raining down like confetti in a parade, Sophie reached down to pick one up as Vernon struck her hand.

"Propaganda!" he yelled, grabbed her and headed for the house.

Spring was slow to come as Sophie thought of the rumors.

Maybe I will be rescued soon. They have to come, they just have to.

"Sophie," Alun said. "Go get the bike and go to town and get our shoes."

Alun knew that the Americans were getting very close and it would be better for Sophie to get caught in town rather than them, being Germans. Sophie set sail down the road, the wind blowing through her hair, as she felt a touch of freedom for once. Seldom was she allowed to go out on her own, but she soon learned of the reasoning for such freedom today. As she reached town, the citizens began to scramble as the all too familiar sounds of B52 Bombers flew overhead. She stopped on the sidewalk, straddling the bike and staring up. She was fearful as she saw again the monsters that would come and eat up the cities, destroying all it came in contact with.

A man suddenly snatched her off the bike and forced her down in an underground room below the buildings. As she huddled again with strangers, her thoughts trailed off to her family. *Are they getting bombed again too? Mother, help me! If it's the Americans, how will they know it's me? I'm Polish.*

"Sit," she said to herself aloud, "Sit."

Smoke filled the air and silence fell on their ears.

"It's over," one said.

Now is the time to get out of here. Sophie jumped up and ran back toward the farm as the earth began to rumble across her path. She dove into a ditch and screamed while covering her head.

"I'm Polish! Don't kill me!" Ammo shot from the fighter planes as smoke boiled up to the heavens. Bombs fell out of the clouds looking like huge eggs pounding to earth. She got up and ran for her life.

I don't want to die alone, not here, she thought.

Coming up on the farm, she met Alun. "Get in the cellar!" He told her as Adelaide cried, kneeling on the first step, and begging for Alun to come inside. He did not want to leave the house. Alun closed the door to the cellar and walked away. As darkness set in, only the sound of heavy breathing could be heard. Others had taken heed to the opened haven from off the street.

A chill went through Sophie's bones from the dampness, the not knowing of who was out there. In a sedated silence, the sultry smell of smoke and gunpowder seared their senses. Talk of the allies throwing hand-grenades in after opening doors to cellars frightened her, but at least she wasn't alone. She sunk ever so deep into the corner of the cellar walls.

SOMEDAY A BLESSING

Slowly, the door opened. As a ray of light angled down toward them, a tall figure could be made out in a halo of smoke. Sophie closed her eyes and drew nearer to the floor. She visualized her parents, her sisters, and her brother for what she thought was the last time.

This is it! Father, Mother, I love you.

Chapter Five
My Angels

Sophie and the others seated beside her took in what could be their last breath of life, peering through squinted eyes as the bright light shined through the now fully swung open cellar door. The silhouette of a soldier came into view at the top of the stairs. A voice called out to them in German, but it was with a different type accent.

"Come out, you will not be hurt," he said.

One by one, everyone crawled up the steps, scared, eyes filled with fear and blinded by the sunlight to the point of pain. Again, encouraged to come out of the cellar by the stranger, Sophie gazed up at a well-dressed American military officer with the sun reflecting off his many badges of honor. Eagle-winged striped patches layered his shoulders. With a firm voice and a stoic expression, he asked each and everyone their nationality.

"Polish. I'm Polish," Sophie said.

He directed her to the left where her eyes met up with a force of men in green surrounding the farm house and barns and some hid in the nearby bushes. Their helmets with a decor of twigs, camouflaged faces, and dust covered green fatigues with heavy belts loaded with artillery. Rifles were slung from their shoulders. Some were chewing gum, something that Sophie had never seen nor heard of, and it looked funny to her at the time. Some sat in groups, tired and weary-

60

SOMEDAY A BLESSING

looking, while others stood guard keeping a watch out for any kind of resistance. Alun was brought out of the house and led toward the group and was asked his nationality.

"German," he replied with his head bowed down.

The high-ranking officer swung back his arm in a back handed motion, but with a hesitation placed his arm back at his side. Sophie caught her breath in a gasp, fearful of Alun's well being. Even though they had kept her captive for five years and worked her without pay against her will, they had become the known. The only existence of any family life she knew, caretakers of her safety, she grew to love them and care for them in an odd sort of way.

Sophie was still unsure of her new captives, so she walked up to the one who seemed in charge and pointed at the ones in the bushes.

"Who are they?" she asked daringly.

"They are the American GIs" he said.

"Am I free?" Sophie hoped.

"Yes, you have been liberated. You are free."

Sophie fell to her knees, leaned over, and kissed the soldier's feet. "You are my angels," she said with tears of joy for the first time in years streaming down her face.

The soldier lifted her up and asked, "Where were you staying?"

"Here on the farm, I've been here for five years."

He motioned for two other soldiers and told them to escort her back to the farm house. As she turned to follow them, he gently touched her arm.

"You don't have to work for the Germans anymore. You are no longer a prisoner of war, but you will need to stay here for a while until we can send you to a displaced person's camp." The news brought an uncertainty to Sophie.

Displaced person's camp? she thought to herself, *When can I go home? How long do I need to stay here?* Sophie had too many questions with no answers. *Maybe the soldiers can tell me more when we get to the house.*

In the kitchen, the two soldiers had a feast. Grabbing the restaurant delicacies, they all sat down at the kitchen table. Sophie

61

joined them, slowly eating, afraid to start a conversation with them. Alun, Adelaide, Vernon, and the three girls walked in the back door, saying nothing as they passed into their living quarters. Sophie felt a given power at that moment, a power as if she was now in control. Not in control of anyone but herself. She would later find that given power was to bring on many new adventures and much heartache. Sophie stared at the two as she finally mustered up the nerve to ask them about going home.

"I would like to go back to Poland," Sophie said softly and quickly, looking back down at the table. She was too fearful to make eye contact.

The two soldiers peered at one another briefly shrugging their shoulders.

"My name is Paul," one said.

Sophie looked up at him with apprehension then realized there was no way she could communicate with them. They could not speak German or Polish and she could not speak English. She stood and walked toward the back porch, feeling an overcoming sleepiness and frustration. She turned toward them and put her hands on her cheek, folded in prayer, signaling that she was going to bed. The two nodded and went back to eating. Paul paused while watching her walk away, feeling compassion for her. He wanted to try to help her. He went out to find someone that could speak German or Polish and brought them back into the house, waking her up. She heard someone speaking German.

"Hey little girl, come down here."

Sophie walked sleepily into the kitchen where a man greeted her in German.

"I'm Troy, nice to meet you," he said, shaking her hand. "You have some questions for me, I hear?"

Sophie had a feeling of importance for the first time since her capture. She was in awe that someone really cared for her concerns about returning home. "I want to go home, back to Poland," she said.

"I see, well, there might be some problems there."

SOMEDAY A BLESSING

Sophie sat down, looking bewildered as Troy continued. "Well, you see, the Russian's have taken over Poland. We're not going there to fight them: we only came to rid Germany of the Nazi regime. A lot of Poles are afraid to go back there. Rumors have it that the Red Army is killing any Poles or Russians that got captured and then worked for the Germans, claiming they have committed treason. We can't help you get back there, either. We can't send you somewhere you may get killed, so you would have to find your own way." Troy spoke further that she would be safer staying in Germany for now, until things settled down.

"We could send you to a displaced person's camp. You will be fed and have a place to sleep…maybe you could even find a job to save some money to go home. I'm sorry I have nothing more to tell you or do for you."

Sophie made the decision to go to the displaced person's camp and Troy said he would work on it, but for her to stay on the farm until she heard from him.

Climbing back up the stairs to her room, Sophie lay down on the bed. She reflected back on the past five years, some memories brought tears and some brought on uncontrollable laughter. She started to laugh about when the milk cows were fed the greens off the tops of the beets and how it would cause them to have diarrhea. When they lifted their tails shamelessly it would squirt out like a fire hose splattering against the barns walls. Shaking her head, she remembered their tails slick and dripping with loose manure. She would try to tie their tails to their legs, fighting every inch of the way, wiggling the tops of their tails until it came loose and slapped her right across the face. She sighed.

I can't believe it, all those years…Vernon chasing me around, almost drowning. All those days spent watching the trains taking people somewhere, somewhere. Wanting to just go home and now I'm free and still can't go home. God, I miss you. I wish I could tell you I'm here and free and ask why the letters stopped coming. It's been years now since I've heard from you all. Her eyes closed. *I*

63

guess it's the Russians now, they stopped all the letters. I don't know what to do, Mother, I don't know what to do.

Drifting off into a slumbered sleep she pondered on the thoughts of Paul and how gentle he was toward her, his smile.

His smile, she thought. *How sweet. I can't believe I'm feeling this way. I wonder what he thinks of me. He has dark hair like the Gypsy lady told me about...hmm...and such blue eyes, too. I wonder...maybe?* She shook her head no. *I don't think so...well...maybe.*

Alun and Adelaide continued working the farm. Vernon would go into the kitchen and see Sophie sitting at the table. "Why don't you help Adelaide in the kitchen? She is working so hard!" Sophie turned around.

"Well, no one helped me all those years! And you can't do anything about it, either! I'm going back to bed!" She stormed out of the room and felt good knowing the American soldiers were still around the farm guarding the power plant across the road. She was free. Now the anger started to fill her heart, no longer feeling for the German family's well-being.

All those years they took from me and now I still can't go home.

In her room, she looked out the window searching through trees and soldiers, attempting to locate Paul amongst them. She spotted him walking up to the back of the farm house.

"Oh my!" Looking quickly at her reflection in the window, she combed her hair and pinched her cheeks to give them a rosy glow. Running down the steps, she paused at the bottom and straightened her dress while striking a pose. Paul walked in with his big smile, making Sophie's heart melt. Troy followed close behind.

"I have a bus ticket for you," he said.

"To where?" she asked, somewhat disappointed that Troy has just interrupted she and Paul's interlude.

"To Simmerhausen. They need help in a hospital there. You interested?"

"Yes! Yes, I am!" She was elated. *I'm leaving this place, finally!*

SOMEDAY A BLESSING

As Troy and Paul let out a laugh at the little girl of 19, Sophie looked at Paul. "Are you going, too? Are you going, too, Paul?" she asked.

Troy interpreted the language as Paul smiled and said, "Tell her I'll be around."

Sophie packed a small bag, leaving her rubber boots leaned up against her bedroom wall. Her heart felt sadness as she looked at them while the morning sun was breaking through the clouds, bringing a warm ray of sunlight into her bedroom window. She thought how she never had seen the sun come in like that. She was always up and out of her room by then, never allowed to return until dark.

I wonder how it would have been if I had just lived here with them, not as prisoner. I think I could have liked it, even Vernon. Things would have been so different. Instead of being choked by Alun that day...I was so scared he was going to kill me. When I took his daughters out sledding, and the oldest girl broke her leg when we ran into that tree, I was so terrified of him. I kept telling him how sorry I was, but he just grabbed my neck, choking and yelling at me. Well, it's all over now. I'm free. As she walked down the steps for the last time, a soldier stood by the back door waiting to take her into town to her bus.

Sophie was dropped off at the bus station, ticket in hand. She stood alone watching people as they calmly greeted each other, friends and family hugging and kissing one another. Timid, she stood, even though this time no one would tell her where to go, or what to do. No guards stood watch over her, yet she stared off in fear and anger as emotions boiled up inside her, thinking how life had just passed her by.

Was anyone even looking for me? Did anyone really care about me? Has anyone been wondering where I am?

She wondered if her own family may have gone on with their own lives. Sophie would learn years later how her mother would stand by the window everyday for hours after her capture. Frank would try to get her to go to bed; she would just shrug him off and say, "I know she

65

will be walking down that road someday. I just know it and I want to be standing right here when she does."

It would be 20 more years before Sophie would walk down that street. She was free, but an iron curtain had fallen between them.

At the bus station, there were ladies in tight skirts wearing lots of lipstick. Their hair never moved in the wind, lacquered with hair spray lying perfectly in curls behind their ears. Sophie looked down at the old tethered pair of shoes she wore the day she was captured, the dress she wore when she was 14.

I'm 19 now and I look like a little girl. Her heart fell apart as she saw herself for the first time, alone, scared, knowing no one. Five years of knowledge lost, her teenage years gone forever while she was working for strangers. She again thought of Paul.

I'm crazy to think he would be interested in me. Look at me...just crazy.

Hearing grinding gears from around the corner, Sophie's body stiffened with a panic feeling that someone may come at her with another pointed gun. The bus rounded the corner and came to a stop. Relieved, she stepped on the bus and soon arrived in front of the hospital.

She soon started a job that paid—cleaning the rooms and changing the bedding for the wounded soldiers. She could not stand to see all the blood and death that surrounded her. Sophie quickly met a new friend and roommate, Helene. They both asked around for other jobs that they could maybe qualify for. Posted on a bulletin board was a sign: "Waitresses Needed" in Rothweston, at an American base.

Sophie and Helene lasted but two weeks at the hospital, then they caught another bus to Rothweston. Sophie could not help thinking that Paul might be there, also. He had stolen her heart that day he escorted her to the farm house. Helene had given her some new hairdo tips and with her first check from the hospital she bought some red lipstick and new clothes. She felt she would look more attractive now if she ever saw him again.

SOMEDAY A BLESSING

Arriving at the base, Helene and Sophie were shown how to make popcorn and carry the trays full of beer mugs. Sophie caught on fast and even picked up some basic English. It seemed that waitressing was right up her alley. She loved to wait on people and clean. Her new bosses welcomed her swiftness and how thoroughly she did her work. Helene and Sophie found a small apartment in Simmerhauson with another waitress. They boarded a bus that would take them back and forth to work. Many American soldiers were on the bus, also. Sophie's eyes scanned through the seats always looking for Paul, and always disappointed in not seeing him. Weeks had passed and Sophie settled in her new job, living on Coca-Cola and popcorn, something she had never had before. She never tired of the smell of popcorn, even after getting so sick from overindulging the snack.

One morning, as she walked into work, she heard a voice call out to her in German. She turned around with a tad of fear hearing her name in German. She saw it was Paul. Her heart jumped as she ran to hug him.

"I thought I would never see you again!" Sophie cried.

Paul lifted her up, somewhat overwhelmed that she reacted with such excitement and swung her around.

"Where have you been?" she asked.

"Around...I've been around," Paul replied. Sophie searched for more of an answer. "I just got stationed here for now. You work here?"

"Yes, now I do. I didn't like the hospital. I've been here for about two weeks. I've been looking all over for you." Sophie hoped he felt the same.

"I see you have learned some English," Paul said surprised. "You must be doing well here and you look good, too!"

There was a pause between them.

"What time do you get off from work?" Paul asked.

"Right now, if I need to!" Sophie glanced at Helene who was grinning at Sophie's desperation for Paul's attention.

Sophie and Paul dated for six months. Sophie fell into a deep love and was on top of the world. Paul was, too, as he sent letters and pictures of the two of them to his family back in the States. His mother started to write Sophie, asking her to come and stay with them. Sophie soon forgot all the pain and loneliness she had felt all those years on the German farm and was ready to start a new life. Sophie wanted so badly to write her family of her new found love and the planning of the trip to the States to meet his family. She continued to work and spent every free moment with Paul. Alone, they took long walks, and he listened intently to her stories. They took the bus to see the cities destroyed from the war. Sophie always wondered how she made it through all this as she hugged Paul, feeling his strength in his arms. She felt safe while he was around. She felt she could never be happier.

One day a bus pulled up as Sophie walked out the canteen's front door to greet Paul, as she always did. This time he walked up to her slowly. She knew right away something was wrong by the expression on his face.

"What is the matter?" she asked. "You're leaving aren't you?" Tears already flooded her eyes.

"Yes, I'm being sent home. I'm sorry." Paul said as he turned around and boarded the bus. Sophie stood speechless, frozen in time. She was in total disbelief and ran after the bus. "Paul! You said you would never leave me! Come back! Take me with you! I'll do anything, please! Please, stop the bus! Come back!" Sophie never knew why he left that day without any explanation. She never heard from him or his family again. Her hopes and dreams once again dwindled before her eyes.

Night fell as she tried to sleep, thinking of all the laughter, the love making, missing his touch.

I don't think I can make it without you. I wish I could tell you how much I need and love you. It is real, so real, God, it hurts so bad, so bad! I don't think I can live through this. God, please send him back to me, please.

Several weeks had passed when Sophie was asked to work in the officers' club where all the high-ranking service men would dine. She thought the change might be what she needed to forget Paul. She

SOMEDAY A BLESSING

called it "the glass house," because of all the windows around the room. She served them already dished up meals from the private kitchen. This time, she was allowed to come out to the fancy dining room. As they sipped their water or wine she would expeditiously refill them, keeping fresh breads in the baskets. She cleared the plates, kept the coffee cups full and hot. She still struggled with her English and the men enjoyed asking her questions just to hear her speak. They loved to tease her. One asked her to greet a Colonel who was approaching the room with, "Good morning, Mister Chicken." Over and over she would say to herself the new words. With a grin, greeting him at the door she spoke loud and precise.

"Good morning, Mister Chicken!"

The room roared with laughter, as she thought it was something cute, but later found out what she had really said. Sophie's feelings were hurt, although it was all in fun. She felt she'd been done in by a soldier already and went back to the base canteen. She spent more and more of her time in bed, until Helene was sick of it.

"Enough is enough! You get out of this bed! You know all these service men do these things. They find a love here, tell you all kinds of things, and then go back to their girlfriends back home. They just leave us, some without even a word...just disappear. At least he came back and told you he was leaving."

Sophie was distraught. "I know, but I love him. I really love him and I know he loves me. I had to have done something wrong...I just don't know what."

Helene grabbed her out of bed. "You're coming with us. The girls and I are going to Rothwesten to the bar. Come on, get ready, and stop wasting your time on that guy."

Dark-haired, with a complexion of his mother's Indian blood to match, his eyes were of sea blue as he gave a noticeable wink toward Sophie. She was unsure of his interest and gave a slight smile back. Her heart already broken once, she was not ready to find herself in another man's arms. She didn't just want to comfort a man's homesickness. She sat down on the bus with her friends. A soldier asked them where they were going.

69

"To town, and you?" Helene answered.

"Yep, that's where we're going." Helene turned, rolling her eyes in doubt. The girls started to laugh. Sophie stared out the window, pretending to watch the passing landscapes. She gave quick glances toward the back of the bus. With each look, the dark-haired man would catch her glances giving a wink. Embarrassed, she turned around, putting her head down, telling herself to just leave it alone. *Don't get caught up in this again,* she told herself.

All getting off the bus, the dark-haired man approached. "I'm Carl," he said, with no response from Sophie. "And you are?"

"Sophie. My name is Sophie," she said looking toward Helene.

Helene nodded to Sophie as if to say *Go ahead, it's alright.*

They group headed to the bar.

The jukebox played as Carl reached for her hand. "Would you like to dance?" he asked her.

Sophie gazed into Carl's mesmerizing steel blue eyes. Her memory of Paul quickly faded and Carl and Sophie seemed to be the only ones in the room. She loved the feel of him embracing her, his hands moved slowly down, caressing the small of her back. In perfect timing, their motions slowed, in unison they stepped to the music. She had never danced other than the polka at home with her family and never wanted this moment to end.

She needed to be loved and cared for. She needed to feel like she was someone. She needed to have someone stay up at night thinking of her. Where is she? What is she doing? She needed to be missed, to be wanted like she thought it was with Paul.

Could this be the moment I have been waiting for? Will he love me forever?

Stanski Family in Holland

Sophie at 14 just before she was kidnapped

Frank and Veronica Stanski

Photo of family in Poznan sent to Sophie while still in captivity

Carl's army locker with Sophie's photo

Sophie during she and Carl's courtship in Germany

Sophie just prior to coming to the United States

Sophie's passport photo

Sophie standing in the doorway of her first home in Arkansas

Sophie and Carl's new home on Pearl Street

The family together after a 20 year separation in 1960

Deborah and Denise hug their mom on her return from Poland in 1960

Sophie in her early 30s after the divorce

Sophie makes contact with her siblings after 26 years of silence

Sophie with her sisters and brother during a reunion in 1986

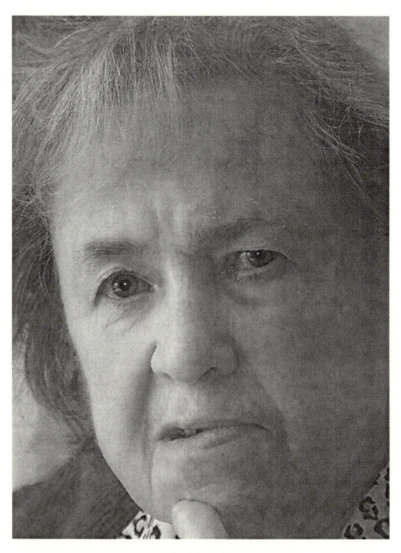
Sophie today

Chapter Six
Crossing Great Waters

Carl and Sophie spent every waking moment together that they could. She had mended her heartbreak from Paul with stitches from Carl. She believed this was her true love. Sophie had discovered she was pregnant with Paul's child when she and Carl became a couple. Carl insisted that Sophie have the child aborted. He was not about to raise another man's baby. Sophie agreed, wanting anything that would make her love happy, even if it was this. He paid for the abortion for Sophie with a carton of cigarettes. The unborn child reminded Sophie of her love for Paul, and she was saddened to discover she was having his child. A part of her wanted to keep the child. Yet another part of her had moved on and she felt she would do anything for Carl. Putting her religious beliefs behind her, she understood why Carl did not want this child. It was not his, but someone else's.

Reluctantly, she agreed to go through with the abortion as she lied down on a dinner table. There was dingy, yellow lighting and a man arrived with a lady assistant. He was dressed in an old dirty hospital gown, stained with blood of other unborn children. Sophie was faced with a decision between morals and survival, something she would find herself faced with throughout her life. She would later regret many choices she had made or allowed others to make for her.

81

Excuses only came from the hopes that God would understand. She rose up off the table after the completion of the procedure, which took a mere ten minutes. She was hurriedly being asked to leave. Bent over in pain, she walked out the front door surprised, to see so many other women waiting outside for their turn. None of them made eye contact with her, each as embarrassed as she of the situation. Alone, she walked back to the bus stop, not sure of what she had just done.

Forgive me, Lord. I am not a terrible person. I will never do this again.

Carl never spoke of what happened when Sophie returned, nor did she. She didn't want to think about it ever again.

One afternoon together on the bus back to Rothweston, Carl leaned over to Sophie. "Will you marry me?" he asked her.

She was speechless.

It was May 1948, and they had been dating steadily for a year now. Carl knew his three years in the United States Air Force would end soon and he would be returning to the United States that winter. Carl and Sophie filled out a four-page questionnaire for the Army's Chaplin. One question listed was "Why do you want to marry him?"

Sophie smiled and simply replied, "Because I love him."

Carl had already been writing his father Jeff for some time, telling him about Sophie. Jeff, through pictures and letters, was developing a deep love and admiration for his future daughter-in-law. Sophie sounded like the type of woman that would be good for his only son. Carl, not yet 21, needed Jeff to write a letter to the U.S. Army inviting them both to live with him and giving Carl his permission to marry Sophie. After months of paperwork, immunizations and medical checkups, Carl and Sophie completed what was required to marry. Along with two other companions, they went to Kassel, Germany, and stood in front of the chaplain giving their vows.

"Through sickness and health, till death do we part."

Sophie held her breath until their "I dos" were complete and the marriage license signed and sealed.

SOMEDAY A BLESSING

On December 13, 1948, in Port Bremen, Haven, Germany, Carl and Sophie set sail on the *William O' Darby*. The ship's hull stood massive out of the ocean water, as it glistened with lights of silver in the sun. Soldiers with their new war brides lined the bows, all waving and saying good-bye to the old lives they were leaving behind. Sophie was six months pregnant with Carl's child by this time and could not help thinking about the gypsy's prediction.

Crossing great waters, she remembered her saying.

For years she wondered how it could possibly happen, and now she was on one of the largest ships, heading for America with a husband and a baby on the way. As the Statue of Liberty gave witness to the soldiers, it also saw the beginnings of new love and hope. Sophie stood in awe staring at Miss Liberty.

What a beautiful sight, she thought, *I've actually made it to the "Land of Milk and Honey."*

This was how it was described to her as a child. As she stepped off the ramps of the ship's bow, she said good-bye to their new-found friends and exchanged names and addresses with promises to keep in touch. Sophie had no idea on this day that a time would come when the "Land of Milk and Honey" would soon turn bittersweet.

Flying home from New York, Carl was glad to be returning to his home town of Jasper, Arkansas. He spent endless days and nights out in the woods of this land with his dogs, exploring caves, searching for arrowheads and fishing. His friends awaited his safe return anxiously. Ted Richmond, an author, was one of his best friends, even though he was old enough to be Carl's father. Ted had brought the first library to the mountains of Newton County. Carl and Ted had spent infinite hours hiking, creating names for the caves they discovered as well as the swimming holes.

Jeff, Carl's father, had found a new wife, Flora, since his return from the Navy. Flora was a very religious lady and believed in working hard and going to church. Jeff had his share of incompatible wives and now he wanted someone who would help him work the farm, someone who would be home to cook and clean for him. Jeff divorced Felicia, Carl's biological mother, and sent his daughter

83

Margaret with her. He kept Carl with him. The kids were only in their pre-teen years at the time. That decision would come back to haunt Jeff in his later years. He always felt guilty for splitting up his children.

Flora never wanted to have children and had never been married before. The two worked the land that Jeff had obtained through a government homestead program in Newton County. They would also commute part of the time to Stillwell, Kansas, where they worked on a horse farm for pay in order to buy supplies for the farm on their return to Jasper. They built a small one-room log cabin to live in while Jeff worked hard building his dream home made of Arkansas stone. The one-room library Ted and Jeff had built was down the hill and was used for the overflow of books from Ted's smaller library. Jeff had stopped drinking and spent his days reading the Bible and working from dawn to dusk.

His father, Harvey Raney, was born in Monroe, Missouri in the late 1800s. He had relocated to Newton County, lived by the Bible, and was true to his wife and family. His teachings of living a God-fearing life led Jeff back to his upbringing of a switch in one hand and a Bible in the other. At one time, Harvey owed the town grocery store $21. He walked to Oklahoma from Jasper to work on the railway for $1 a day. He stayed for 30 days, receiving $30, then returned to pay his debt of $21 and had $9 to spare.

"A mans word is his only honor," he used to say.

Jeff was looking forward to having Carl back home in hopes of rebuilding a good father-son relationship. Jeff drove to Springfield, Missouri, to pick them up while Carl's great-grandparents waited for the war bride to arrive. Sophie was excited to meet this new family. She loved Carl and the fact that she was rescued out of the now-devastated Europe. Carl and Sophie had spoke of plans to send for her father and mother when they settled in. Her dreams were finally coming true, almost too fast and too real.

Sophie was in awe during the drive from the Springfield Airport and across the Arkansas state line. The beautiful pine trees lining the

SOMEDAY A BLESSING

curving roads were breathtaking. She could not wait to see where she and Carl would be spending their lives together.

They arrived and spent their first night with Carl's grandparents, Harvey and Alice. Sophie fit right in immediately. The entire family wanted to hear about the war, her life in Poland, her family, the kidnaping. Hours filled with conversations and home-grown foods from the farm and the large family gave her a sense of acceptance. Sophie, though disappointed about her new home, did not say a word to Carl. The home had no running water and no inside facilities. She never dreamed that people in the United States still had to live like this.

Carl was receiving very little money from the military and Sophie received about $150 a month government monies as a war bride's temporary assistance. The newlyweds did not have the money to rent or buy a home, so Harvey insisted they stay with them. Sophie adored Harvey and Alice, and pitched right in helping around the house. Alice had given birth to 13 children and was well aware of the needs of a young pregnant woman. Sophie felt comfortable around Carl's grandparents and her first born child would end up becoming Alice's favorite until the day she died.

One day, as Sophie walked around to the back of the house looking for Carl, out the back door came a rain shower of urine. Alice, holding a bucket, stood looking sorrowfully as Sophie wiped the smelly yellow fluid from her face. She quickly noticed the odor ascending from the ground around the back door. Instead of going to the outhouse at night, they would place a bucket in the corner of the bedroom and pitch it outside the back door in the morning. Sophie quickly headed down to the Buffalo River to bathe, scrubbing herself to the bone!

The next day, Harvey was cleaning out from under the outhouse. Sophie was on her way down to the creek to do laundry with a scrub board and a hand-made bar of lye soap when she turned just in time to see Harvey taking the feces to the garden area. She couldn't believe her eyes as she watched in horror while Harvey threw the human waste all over the garden. She started her starvation plan again. It made her sick to her stomach, the thought of eating anything coming from that garden again.

Standing by the stream, picking the ticks off her and swatting at the gnats flying into her eyes and around her face, she began to wonder how she had come to this. She was working harder and living in the same conditions as she did in Poland and Germany...maybe even worse.

What kind of life has he brought me to? she asked herself.

She finally mustered up the courage to complain to Carl about their living conditions. She told him she was unhappy living this way and she didn't think she could take it much longer. Carl, in an attempt to make Sophie happy, bought an old Ford pick-up truck with Sophie's war money and they moved to his father's farm.

Ted's one-room log cabin built for the library books sat empty at that time and as Carl backed the truck up to the front door, Sophie about fainted.

Oh no! she thought, *Not again, it's the same darn thing.*

No running water, in the corner stood an old wood stove with a cardboard box full of kindling. A metal poster bed with a dingy, worn feather mattress was tucked in the corner behind the door. Two chairs around a small square hand-made wooden table painted in white wash and one set of dresser drawers were the only decor. The walls were covered with wall paper over cardboard boxes that had been nailed to the walls with roofing nails. The outhouse, lined with cob webs and wasp nests, sat between the two cabins by the goat shed. Sophie was due in March the next year and it was all she could do to keep herself warm that winter. She would attempt to keep the cabin clean by sweeping the floor every day, sometimes more often. She would hang the few throw rugs on a line and beat them with a broom handle to get rid of all the dust as best she could. She hated living there, but at least she and Carl were alone together.

Carl had not found work as of yet, not really knowing what he wanted to do. With everyone giving him advice, it was easier for him to do nothing and just go fishing. He had thoughts of going to school. His uncle Oliver, who was a physician, suggested he go to medical

SOMEDAY A BLESSING

school. They continued to live off of Sophie's government subsidy even though her benefits would run out soon. Jeff and Flora spent all their time working and clearing the land. Flora had a wonderful garden and they didn't use the outhouse for fertilizer. Jeff milked goats and two milk cows and sold the milk for income. Flora and Sophie would sit outside on the chairs under the pine trees churning the cream for butter and breaking green beans for supper. Sophie liked the farm, despite the conditions. She loved spending time with Jeff and Flora and the other relatives that came to visit.

Irma, Carl's Aunt, took Sophie under her wing. Sophie could do no wrong in her eyes. Irma showed her how to live the old southern country life as best she could. Irma tried to explain to Sophie how to bake a blackberry pie to surprise Carl, as it was his favorite. Sophie had never even heard of a blackberry pie in her life. When she made the pie, she squeezed the juice out of the berries and all that was left were the seeds. She thought it looked funny but finished the pie and was proud of her accomplishment. When Carl took his first bite, he started laughing.

"How in the world did you manage to bake this horrible tasting pie?" he asked her.

Sophie was so embarrassed when Irma told her what she had done wrong. "Sophie, you don't squeeze the juice out of the berries, you leave them whole, you silly girl. I'm sorry, Sophie. I should have helped you with the pie." Irma laughed and this would be a family joke for many years to come.

When Sophie would cook meals for her new family she would have two kinds of potatoes, four vegetables and two meats, enough to feed an army. Food portion adjustment was hard for her since she had to cook for so many people in Germany. Jeff and Flora were extremely thrifty and having so many leftovers frustrated Flora, especially since they had no where to store them. Flora could be caught sometimes stuffing her mouth with some of the leftovers before dumping them into the bucket for the pig's slop. She hated to see so much food go to waste.

Carl and Sophie pitched in and helped with the farm work for free rent and food. Sophie, again, was becoming disgruntled living in the cabin and began to complain to Carl. She once again built up enough courage to tell Carl that she refused to live there any longer and bring their first born child into that cabin. It was not what she wanted and had hopes that Carl would want more also. She felt life there was a choice, not a given. Even though Carl felt comfortable with their lifestyle on the farm, he knew he had an obligation to make Sophie happy.

In the early spring, they loaded up and moved to Russellville, Arkansas, where they rented a small trailer house, about the same size of the cabin they had just moved out of. Carl chose Russellville because there was a college there and his Aunt and Uncle lived nearby also. Sophie felt it would be better for now; at least the trailer had running water and an indoor bathroom. Carl's Aunt Doris lived close by and he quickly found some new fishing buddies. Sophie stayed at home and Carl continued his life as usual, still unemployed. He did make the decision to go to college. Sophie found some houses to clean for extra money while awaiting the birth of their child. Carl began to spend more and more time away from home. Late night fishing trips turned into all-nighters as Sophie's due date grew near. Sophie had befriended Carl's aunt and a neighbor, with so many nights spent alone. She was happy to have friends close by to talk to, although she wished her mother were there to help her through this pregnancy and birth. Carl's Aunt Doris was very supportive, but she wasn't mother. Sophie would lay awake at night feeling the movement of the life inside her.

Mother, Stasia, Krystyna, Zenon, and Father…oh how I wish you were here or me there. I miss you all so much. When will I see you all again? I feel so alone. I'll be having your grandchild any day now. When will you see the baby? When? When will you ever see this baby?

The night finally arrived when Sophie's water broke. She called out to Anita, her new friend and neighbor, but found the only one home was Joe, Anita's husband.

SOMEDAY A BLESSING

"Where's Carl?" he asked her.

Sophie, fighting the pain of labor replied, "He went fishing, you know, where he always goes his favorite spot."

Sophie gave birth that night to a healthy baby boy she named Daryl. Carl had never arrived at the hospital for the birth. As she lay on a hospital bed holding her new infant, she wondered where Carl could be. Joe had come up during the night stating he could not find Carl at his usual fishing hole. Sophie was getting angrier by the minute. Carl had been performing this disappearing act almost every night and so had Anita. She decided she was going to leave him and go back to Poland as soon as she got out of the hospital.

When Carl finally made it to the hospital, he could sense Sophie's anger and disappointment the moment he entered the room. She held Daryl as she glared at him.

"I'm leaving you as soon as I get out of this hospital!"

"Where do you think you're going to go?" Carl asked her as he reached to hold his son.

"Back to Poland. My family will help me. I don't have to live like this," Sophie said. "And where were you last night anyway? Joe went looking for you at the fishing hole and you weren't there."

Carl was infuriated. She could tell by the look on his face. "I was there dammit! Joe just didn't look in the right spot!" He defended himself.

The next day Sophie was discharged from the hospital and Carl, like a doting husband, was there to pick up his wife and newborn son.

The days that followed tended to become tumultuous at times. Carl and Sophie were arguing more often, and he refused to give up his "fishing trips." He was skipping classes at school and continued to not work or help make a living. Sophie was taking care of the house and the baby and soon returned to cleaning houses for income, taking Daryl with her since she could not afford to pay someone to watch him.

After an argument, Carl stomped out of the house with a small suitcase filled with clothing. "I'm going to Roy and Minta's in Texas. You can have this place," he yelled.

Carl drove to Texas to his aunt and uncle's house, a good eight-hour drive, only to find that they were not home. They had gone on vacation. Carl slept in his car and waited for them to return, not knowing they would be gone for weeks. He wandered around Dallas for a week, too proud to return home to Sophie and having to admit he couldn't make it without her. While he was gone, Sophie felt relieved. She continued working and saving every dime she could. It was a relief not having to wonder or worry where Carl was, when or if he was coming home.

She packed her bags and prepared to leave Carl. At that point, she didn't know exactly how, but she was going to find a way back home to Poland. She didn't want to be there if and when Carl came back home.

All dressed up, Carl popped in the door a few days later. "Where do you think your going?" he asked Sophie.

Not looking at him, he grabbed her dress and ripped the shoulder a tad.

"Back to Poland!" she screamed. "You are not going to treat me like this!" She was shocked that he had returned so soon. "I thought you were leaving me," she said.

"No, and you're not going, either. I've decided we're moving to Kansas City. I'm going to join the National Guard there and there's more work available, also. We need to get out of Arkansas anyway."

Sophie found herself torn again between her marriage and Poland. She had been writing her parents telling them how wonderful it was being in the United States, but so far it had not been so great. She felt hypocritical in her writings. Carl was cheating on her, she suspected, from the long all-night fishing trips. They were living in a small trailer and Carl had no work, her new grandparents' lifestyles were far from the way she pictured life in the States would be. She did not really want to go back to Poland nor be a failure at her first marriage. Therefore, she reluctantly agreed to go to Kansas City, hoping and praying things would get better.

Maybe if Carl gets a job his time will be occupied and he'll settle into the family, she thought.

SOMEDAY A BLESSING

Sophie wanted things, nice things, and did not feel guilty for wanting them. She just knew that this time her home, keepsakes, and her life would not be taken from her. She was in the United States, wasn't she?

Chapter Seven
The Neighborhood

Within a few years after moving to Kansas City, Carl found a good job at the Ford Motor Company in Claycomo, Missouri. Quickly afterward, he was promoted to Foreman and before Sophie knew it, they were able to afford to buy their dream home. Sophie and Carl by this time had three of their four children: Daryl, 6; David, 4; and Deborah, 2.

The boys had dark hair with rounded faces accented with blue eyes, just like their dad. Deborah was small framed like her mother, blond curls and blue eyes. Sophie was excited to have her two boys and a daughter. She was hoping the one she carried now would be a girl also. It would round out her family the way Carl had once spoke of. He wanted to name all their kids with their first name starting with "D."

"Let's have the boys first and then the girls. The boys will be able to protect the girls when they get older," he had once said.

If Sophie could have anything to do with it, she would hope and pray for just that...anything to complete she and Carl's happiness.

After searching for the perfect place to raise their family, Carl and Sophie settled on a new housing addition, Edgewood Park in Independence, Missouri. The homes were lined up, so similar to one another, and yet just different enough to attract all buyers. Some of

SOMEDAY A BLESSING

the homes had basements while others did not. Two and three-bedroom homes stood waiting for new families. The yards were postage stamps in appearance with freshly-laid green plush sod. The driveways sparkled with white, clean gravel.

In a dream come true, they selected a home that was within walking distance of the new Ott Elementary grade school. New neighbors, new houses, and new friends...life was coming together. Everything was new, including their fourth child, a daughter they named Denise. It was done, and the camera's shutter was never wasted. Many pictures were taken of the boys and girls together and sent to family and friends.

The home Sophie and Carl selected was a quaint three-bedroom, one-bath ranch style home with a basement and a yard ready for fencing. The kitchen had bright yellow cabinets, the floors were hardwood. The main thing was that everything was new. Sophie was not just excited about having a house, but a new house at that. There were no attached memories related to this house, only new ones to be made.

Carl soon obtained good credit and, shortly after purchasing the home, they began to furnish it with beautiful new furniture and appliances. Living room furniture, a new stove and refrigerator, new bedroom furniture—everything that anyone could ever want, Sophie now had. Her family that was still struggling in Poland behind the iron curtain would be so proud of her. She just knew she would soon be able to help them out with any needs they would have.

She spent many hours a day making sure that her home was spotless. The hardwood floors would be hand waxed and polished every month on her hands and knees. Sophie applied Johnson Wax with a rag in a circular motion until all the floors surfaces were covered. After the wax had dried, Sophie would then begin the chore of polishing the floors to a beautiful shine by hand. She never minded this job: it was her home and she was used to hard work.

It was several years before Carl purchased Sophie an electric buffer for Christmas to help her keep her floors shiny and new looking. Everyone said she had the best looking floors in the entire neighborhood, and she did. The children enjoyed sliding down the hallway in only their socks on the slickly polished floors running into their mother and father's bedroom door that they used for a stopper.

Carl and Sophie also soon had a new car, a Ford Station Wagon. Shortly after purchasing the car, they added a shiny new red and white speed boat. Sophie, Carl, and the children were often seen pulling off in the All-American Dream with their new boat and car. Off to the lake they would go for a day of swimming and water skiing. Sophie never wanted to learn to water ski, possibly stemming from her near drowning experience in Germany, but she was content driving the boat for her husband as he sped through the wake on his skis. She was thrilled to see her husband and children happy.

Sophie was content simply taking care of her family. Like her mother, Veronica, her family came first. Carl would want for nothing. The house was spotless, the kids always safe and clean. On his return from work, dinner was always ready and on the table. Sophie always kept her self immaculate and would wait on Carl when he got home from work, taking his shoes off, rubbing his feet, and putting house slippers on him.

Carl, still having a bit of Arkansas country boy in him, would go down the Missouri river to fish. Running into a man named Conrad, who had puppies to give away, he thought what a nice addition to the family a dog would be. Even more interesting about these pups was the fact that they were part wolf. Queenie became the newest member of the family. She took it in stride as she would grab the kids' feet and ankles trying to drag them through the tall grass left unmowed in the far back of the yard for her to hide in. The kids would sit out three metal lawn chairs in a clover leaf shape and dare each other to get from one to the other before Queenie got their legs. The neighbor kids soon joined the so-called fun. As she got older, she started to draw blood from the children, but the fear was overcome by their child-like ways and love for the dog. By the time Queenie was full grown, she weighed around 100 pounds.

One day, while playing in the backyard and rough housing with her as usual, Deborah began running from Queenie, only to fall to the

SOMEDAY A BLESSING

ground. Queenie quickly pounced on her face with one of her claws, narrowly missing her eye. Bleeding, she ran to the house crying. It was soon after when all the fun ended.

While on a trip to Arkansas to visit Jeff and Flora, Carl had instructed his neighbor Bud Smith to get rid of the dog while they were away. They were becoming concerned about her growing viciousness toward the kids. She was soon replaced with a new dog they named Tippy. Deborah would always feel guilty that she was the reason they had to get rid of Queenie, and her brothers would never let her forget it, either.

Sophie and Carl were the envy of the neighborhood, at least by some, anyway. Like sheep in wolves clothing, some of the other wives would become more than envious about this new family in the neighborhood, to the point of wanting what Sophie had: not her home, but her husband.

Directly across the street from Sophie's haven moved a family that included Peg, her husband Willie, and their three children.

Peg was a dark-haired, brown-eyed, somewhat attractive woman and she had a way of making all the women and men in the neighborhood a little uncomfortable. She had a loud laugh that seemed to want to catch everyone's attention. The clothes she wore were of a seductive style: low-shouldered blouses and form-fitting knickers. She battled with her weight mostly because of the fact she was short in stature, maybe 5' 4", but her battle of the bulge would not stop her from getting what she wanted. She had two things going for her: her smile and her laughter. She could be whatever you wanted her to be. Peg's husband Willie was an average looking man, tall, thin and very quiet. He worked everyday to support his family and basically that was about it. Sophie and Peg would speak on occasion; however, it was usually Peg initiating the occasional neighborly chit chat. Often, Sophie would see Peg on her lawn recliner out in the front yard during the hot humid summers sunbathing, scantily clad in her bikini. Sophie noticed it was more and more often during the time Carl arrived home from work. As soon as Carl would drive up, Peg would then strut into the house and would begin playing her piano as

95

loud as she could, facing the always opened front door. By early summer, Peg had a dark, sultry tan and made sure she wore as much white as possible in her clothing in order to make herself look even darker. The neighborhood children used to tease that Peg was half "nigger" because she would get so dark. Peg quickly became acquainted with Lilly two houses north of her. Lilly, unbeknownst to Peg, also had her eye on Carl.

Lilly resided with her husband Ronald and their three boys. She was a feisty, red-haired woman that found it hard to keep her mouth shut. She loved to gossip and instigate turmoil in the neighborhood, so she and Peg hit it off right away. Since most of the women in the neighborhood did not work, they had plenty of time to nose around and get into other people's affairs.

Lilly's husband was a plain, tall, skinny, blond-haired man. He was quiet and very submissive to his wife. Lilly definitely wore the pants in the family. Rumor had it that she made her husband sit down to urinate so that he wouldn't get urine on the floor.

Peg and Lilly would burn up the phone lines talking about various neighbors, always ending up with their favorite topic, Carl and Sophie. They often enjoyed talking about how handsome Carl was with his southern twang, dark complexion, and those gorgeous blue eyes. Seldom was he ever in a bad mood as he would smile at all the neighbors when he passed them by. As for Sophie, she found herself in her own little world. She was completely satisfied with just her home and family. She was not concerned about other people's lives. She was always busy maintaining her home and children and keeping everything impeccably clean. Sophie would often write letters to Carl's family, her family, and friends. Sophie was totally in the dark when it came to Peg's devious plans.

Sophie received a letter from a friend.

December 3, 1955
My dear Sophie,
    Thanks a lot for your very nice letter. I was surprised to have one so soon from you. Yes, we have not forgotten you

SOMEDAY A BLESSING

and we always think of you. We do look at the pictures you have sent, and can not believe that Debra is so fast on her feet. I can imagine, Sophie dear, that you have a lot of work to do because of four children. I would really like to see your family. Why didn't Carl stay in the army? Would it not of been better for all of you if could come back to Germany to stay for two years like your husband's cousin did? I bet you would have a good time, don't you think?

But who knows with your past experiences you had. You can still be happy, because you have so many things that we haven't, and never will be able to get. I mean a TV and car. In the States, almost everyone has a car. MY son Heinz is trying to come to the States also, and will come and visit you and your family. Merry Christmas.

Your friend,
Aneliers

Peg and Lilly began to make friends with Sophie and would often drop over unannounced inviting Sophie and Carl out on weekends with their husbands. The three couples could be seen many weekends out on the town, just a group of good friends it seemed, neighbors getting to know each other and having a good time.

Peg and Lilly would tend to get a little tipsy during the evening and soon they would get loose-lipped and flirty. Since Carl did not allow Sophie to drink or smoke, she never got the little buzz that maybe would have made her overlook the flirtatious nuances made toward her husband. Sophie felt secure in her marriage, and while driving her slightly drunken husband home from these parties she found confirmation of her peace and security in their conversations.

"Those women are such sluts," Carl would say.

Sophie's sense of security came from the feeling that her husband would never want anything to do with Peg or Lilly by the way he was always putting them down.

The partying was not enough for Peg. She would make sure that she was out sunbathing every time Carl was outside, washing the car

97

or doing yard work. Of course, Carl noticed the voluptuous woman across the street. How could he not? He was a red-blooded American male.

Sophie watched cautiously as Peg would promenade in front of her husband. As much as Sophie was busy taking care of the house and being a good wife, Peg's antics did not go unnoticed. She often wondered why Carl would insist that she take one of the children with her every time she went to the grocery store and why he would never allow her to wear shorts on those trips. She knew that Carl enjoyed looking at attractive women and she knew he enjoyed sneaking peeks at Peg in her bikini. Sophie had a great body, and she knew so.

Why doesn't he want to see me dressed that way? she wondered.

Her thoughts always returned to those times that Carl would insinuate that Peg and Lilly were simply sluts and how he couldn't believe their husbands allowed them to act and dress the way they did. Carl had even once said to her that if Marilyn Monroe walked by him he would never leave her. She felt secure in what he said to her, but very unsure of his actions.

Life in the new neighborhood all seemed surreal to her. She had never been happier in her life, happy like she was in Holland. Only this time she had the man the gypsy had told her she would meet and the children the gypsy had predicted.

How strange, she thought, *how could this ever end? I have finally received my blessing in life, a blessing for all my trials and tribulations of being a prisoner of war. It is now all worth it. I am truly blessed.*

Chapter Eight
The Affair

Sophie continued to remain in contact with her parents and siblings via telephone and letters. She was excited about the possibility of her chance to visit them soon and seeing them again for the first time in the 20 years since her abduction. It was now 1960. Life in Sophie's eyes couldn't seem any better. Her husband had a well-paying job; she had a beautiful home and children.

Divorce was almost an unheard of thing in 1960. Life was simple. The nightly news was on 15 minutes each night, and there was not a lot of news to report. Crime rate was low and only the Charlie Starkweather's and "In Cold Blood" infamous murders made the big news. Every night after the 10:00 p.m. news, the 10:15 movie would begin. The children were in bed and it was time for Sophie and Carl to spend some quality time together. Their sex life was good, or so she thought. Sophie was there whenever her husband needed her. She knew how to be a good wife, and most importantly, she wanted to be.

Sophie and Carl planned her reunion trip back home to Poland. Excitement filled the air as she bought the airline tickets that would take her and her oldest child, Daryl, to Poland. The trip was planned to a tee. The Worlds Fair was in Warsaw, Poland, that year and it would allow visitors to enter Poland, even though they were still

99

behind the iron curtain for the first time since the war. Sophie's parents Veronica and Frank waited with much anticipation for her arrival. Veronica was almost sick waiting to see Sophie. She had cried so many nights for her daughter. Soon she would be able to hold and kiss her again. Her sisters and brother were excited, also. They all had families of there own now, so much had happened since Sophie had disappeared.

Will seven weeks be long enough to talk about so much? she wondered.

Carl had Lonnie and Chuck Wilson, their next door neighbors, care for the other three children while he took Sophie and Daryl to the airport. It was a big thing in the neighborhood, and the entire city of Independence for that matter. Everyone had heard Sophie's story. It was also in the Ford Motor company newsletter with a picture of Carl and Sophie sitting on the living room couch planning for the trip. Bud and Donna Smith would accompany Carl and Sophie to see them off. While at the airport, Sophie received a delivery of a dozen of the most beautiful red roses. Believing they were from Carl, she opened the card.

Have a Wonderful Trip. Love, Peg and Lilly, the card read.

Trying to find the good in this gesture, she could not help feeling something was up. She never really felt she had anything in common with Lilly and Peg and was always suspicious that something was going on between the both of them and Carl. Soon after receiving her roses, Peg and Lilly showed up at the airport out of the blue, seemingly so excited for Sophie. What a coincidence! They gave hugs and kisses to everyone there, wishing Sophie nothing but the best!

Sophie was homesick for her family even before the plane ever lifted off the ground. Her sixth sense was in overload, too, as the rain started to pour.

Something just isn't right, she couldn't help from thinking, *Why are Lilly and Peg so happy to see me leave?*

Her thoughts even entertained the idea of the trip being cancelled because of the rain. It was a bad omen to fly in the rain, she had heard.

SOMEDAY A BLESSING

Sophie was such a homebody, she never liked change and once in her comfort zone, it was difficult to leave it. She kept the thoughts of her parents and siblings in her mind. She knew she needed to see them as much as they needed to see her, she only wished her entire family was with her.

Carl and Sophie's neighborhood friends watched as her plane lifted off and soared into the cloud-covered sky. The chatter continued as they all walked back to their cars to return home. Carl knew the other children were waiting for his return and he needed to be there for them. He picked the children up from Lonnie's and returned home. It was different with Sophie not there. Carl prepared the children supper. The kids—then 8, 6, and 4—complained because the potatoes still had some of the skins on them when he presented them with their first meal prepared by their father.

"Mother never fixes them like this. We don't like potatoes with skin on them," Deborah said.

"Well, too bad, you eat them or you go hungry," Carl replied.

The children ate the potatoes and left a small pile of skins on their plates. Carl was frustrated; however, he did the best he could. He was pretty proud of himself. He fed the kids, gave them baths and got them to bed, all on his own. He missed Sophie and Daryl; however, he was happy that he was able to give this trip to his wife.

Sophie called Carl the next day to let him know she and Daryl arrived safely, and spoke of how much she missed everyone. She went on about her family and how happy they were to see her and her of them. She hung up reluctantly and continued on with her family reunion. She clung to the fact that she would be back home in America soon. The seven weeks would pass quickly she hoped and she would be back to her husband, her life.

Sophie never left her mother or father's side, listening to all the war stories, as they all cried together. She found out how Zenon was beaten for losing a set of keys and jumped through a window, only to be met by more Nazi's, beating him even more. Her two uncles, Leon and Stanley, were hung for working for the underground newspaper. She learned how her mother stood by the window for hours on end looking for her to return home, how she just knew that one day she would see Sophie walking down the lane toward her home. When Veronica passed away some years later, her family always said she died from a broken heart because Sophie had always been her favorite daughter. With her family now living in a cramped three room apartment, Sophie felt guilty, for how she had so much. She vowed that she would help her family out of poverty as soon as she got back to the States. She promised them.

Back in the States that evening, there was a knock at Carl's door. There stood Peg dressed in tight white knicker pants and a tight-fitted knit sweater. She smiled big, showing off her pearly whites.

"Do you need any help Carl? I just wanted to come over to see if you needed any help with the children, cooking, or any housework with Sophie gone and all."

Carl told Peg he was doing okay but was glad she came over.

"Come on in," he said.

Peg stepped into the house, looking around sheepishly to see where the kids were.

"The kids are in the backyard playing," Carl said.

"Oh," Peg perked up.

She was hoping that all her seducing ways would pay off as she started having a funny feeling in her stomach being alone with Carl for the first time. A streak of jealousy stirred up inside her as she looked around another woman's home, struck with envy that it was not she, but Sophie, living here with Carl.

Peg had long lost any feelings for her husband way before ever seeing Carl. Willie was a heavy beer drinker and would meet his buddies almost every night after work. Peg used this as a strategy to hold late night conversations in Carl's home while Sophie was gone.

Carl and Peg sat down on the sofa and began to converse. Peg knew she was ready to make a move on Carl, but she had to be careful. After all, both of them were married.

She continued talking with Carl, making him seem that she was genuinely interested in his life, Sophie, and his children. Carl enjoyed the fact that this woman listened to him, a set of new ears to talk to. It didn't hurt that she dressed provocatively and had a great body either. Cheating on Sophie had not been new to Carl, he had cheated on her before, but this time, there were neighbors and friends all keeping an eye on him. He had to be careful...this time.

Lonnie babysat the Raney kids while Carl went to work. With Peg's husband working many late hours and partying with his buddies, it made it even more convenient for her trips to visit Carl when he arrived home from work. During the day, Peg burned up the telephone wires and visited Lilly often to talk about her school-girl crush on Carl. Lilly was a tad bit jealous when she would visit Carl with Peg, she had noticed that Carl seemed a bit smitten with Peg, too. Lilly had a secret crush on Carl herself, but soon found herself as only a confidant for Peg.

During the first few weeks after Sophie's departure, Peg continued to go in for the kill, always showing the good side of herself, continuing to tell Carl of her troubles with Willie. Carl in return would tell Peg that he never really loved Sophie, but just felt sorry for her, being pregnant and all when they were in Germany. Carl would never tell Peg of the undertaking it had been getting Sophie to the United States. Now that Carl was smitten with Peg, Sophie was only becoming an obstacle. Carl began to paint a horrid picture of Sophie to Peg.

"She was screwing every soldier that came around. I even had to pay for an abortion for her," he said.

"Well, you deserve better than that," Peg said, delighted to hear of the dysfunction of what she thought was a perfect family.

Peg would try to confirm Carl's thoughts of all the women during war time just wanting to find an American soldier to trap into marriage for a free trip to the States. By the time the seven weeks were up, Peg did just that. Before indulging in sex for the first time, the verbal bashing of their mates would somehow make it seem right. They were two mistreated human beings, being used by ones who loved them.

Like a bird with a broken wing, Sophie, thousands of miles away, would read between the lines of their brief telephone conversations that seemed to be coming few and far between. Carl was calling in sick to work often and the last time he talked to her he mentioned taking the kids to Arkansas. Carl had already called his dad, Grandpa Jeff, and told him he was having a hard time taking care of the kids, the house, and working while Sophie was away. Jeff told him to bring them down to the farm. He would love to take care of them and he would bring them back when Sophie returned from Poland. Jeff thought Carl had only the best intentions for the kids. The thought of the marriage being threatened never crossed his mind. That weekend, Carl packed up the kids and drove them to Jasper where they would spend the next month.

Carl was now free as a bird to carry on his love affair with Peg, no wife or kids around, he felt like a single man. Under the watchful eye of the neighbors, some were becoming suspicious of Carl and Peg spending so much time together. Willie was oblivious to it all, working hard late hours. Lilly was their cover-up, but Carl knew they needed to become a little more secretive. He wasn't stupid: he was an expert at having affairs and never really getting caught.

After Carl got home from work, he showered and soon was seen leaving the house. About five to ten minutes later, Peg found a reason to go on an errand and would leave her house. At a small park at the Missouri River near 291 Highway, Carl waited. Peg drove up and got into Carl's car. They immediately started making out and talked of their spouses on through the night. There was never any real talk of them leaving their spouses for each other, but they were having an increasingly difficult time being away from one another.

Carl knew their time together was running short. Sophie would soon return, but the love affair had grown so out of control, he wasn't sure if he even cared for Sophie anymore. The kids were tearing him up at the time, just the thought of having to leave them. Peg ensured him that there was no reason that he would have to ever lose them and she offered to help all she could. By this time, she was in dire need to hook him. She worried when Sophie returned he might end this affair. She was in love with him and with a compassionate deceit she would tell him all that he wanted to hear. The errors of their ways

SOMEDAY A BLESSING

would soon send the whole neighborhood and two families clashing into a who's who.

Talk amongst the neighbors continued to grow. Everyone knew something was going on between Peg and Carl, even though they thought their little secret was so well kept. Sophie was to return home the next day and Peg was out of her mind! She called Carl, frantically begging him to be with her. She wanted him to know that she couldn't live without him and made him promise not to make love to anyone but her. Carl felt the same about Peg, and they met again that night at the riverside to make love one more time.

Grandpa Jeff packed up the three children along with their cousin, Drucella, and started the drive back to Independence to welcome Sophie and Daryl back home. It was a six or seven hour drive, so the kids made beds in the back of the pick-up truck. Jeff put a camper shell on as the kids played on the blankets, excited to see their father and mother. Carl was on his way to the airport, awaiting Sophie and his son's arrival.

Nervously pacing back and forth near the gate, Carl wondered if he would be able to cover up his guilty conscience. Would Sophie notice his distance? The plane arrived at the gate as scheduled and Carl watched as passenger after passenger departed through the exit gates. Finally, he saw Sophie and Daryl. Sophie spotted Carl and a huge smile crossed her face. She was ecstatic to see him again. Her pace picked up as she made her way through the crowd, holding onto Daryl's hand in order not to lose him. She put her arms around Carl's neck and kissed him softly, telling him how much she missed him and how happy she was to see him. He hugged her back and quickly focused his attention on Daryl, giving his boy a hug and started asking about his trip and the plane ride.

As they waited at the turn stile for Sophie's luggage, the talk was about the trip.

"How were your parents? Did you have a great time?"

Carl wanted to be sure that he had provided Sophie with something pleasurable in her life; he thought he owed her that. He knew that Peg was at home waiting for them to arrive and that she would be watching his every move.

Sophie excitedly told Carl how much she wanted to help her family now that she was back home. "They have so little, honey. I told them that maybe we could send them some money to help get them a bigger apartment. Don't you think we can?" She asked Carl.

"Mmmhmm." Carl replied, only wanting to appease her.

Carl had Sophie and Daryl wait at the curb with the luggage while he went to get the car. He pulled up to the curb, loaded the luggage and they started their drive home. Sophie was talking a mile a minute, so excited. She had to tell him everything. As she told Carl all about her trip, turning onto their street she noticed tears running down his face. She did not want to embarrass him by saying anything, so she continued with her stories.

He must have really missed me. They must be tears of joy, she thought.

When Jeff arrived with the children, there was already a party going on. The house was filled with friends, neighbors and the Press. It seemed EVERYONE was there for this welcome home party, including Peg and Lilly. The children quickly ran into the house and hugged their mother. Deborah, who seemed to be the most homesick, cried and climbed into Sophie's lap, refusing to leave that haven for fear her mother would disappear again. Soon all the other children were running and playing with the neighborhood kids. Everything appeared happy again.

The party went on it seemed for hours as Sophie told everyone everything about her trip. Carl and Peg glanced at each other occasionally, a quick smile, a flirty pout, making sure not to be caught by any of the other party goers. As everyone began to leave the party, Sophie was drained. There was plenty of food left over, so she did not have to cook dinner. She gathered her children around her, so happy to see them all, so happy to have her family together again. She was finally home, her real home. Carl and Sophie got the kids rounded up for baths and goodnights. Jeff and Drucella were getting ready to head back.

SOMEDAY A BLESSING

"I've got cows to milk in the morning," he said.

While Carl was tucking the kids in bed, the phone rang. Sophie went to answer, only to hear the click of a hang up.

Hmm... she wondered, *who in the world would call this late at night and then hang up? It must have been a wrong number.*

A short time later the phone rang again, this time Carl answered.

"Oh hi, Fred," he said.

The conversation then became a lot of "yes" and "no" answers.

"Okay. I will."

He hung up the phone a short time later, explaining that it was one of his friends from work. Unbeknownst to Sophie, it had been Peg, crying uncontrollably in the phone.

"I can't stand this! You have to promise me, Carl, that you won't have sex with her tonight, promise me!" she had said.

Sophie and Carl retired to the bedroom. She had long anticipated this reunion with her husband. She was tired from the trip but was sure Carl would need her tonight. She waited anxiously for her husband to undress and join her under the covers. As Carl climbed into bed and placed his arms around Sophie, she snuggled into him as close as she could get.

"I missed you so much, Carl."

"I'm glad your home, too."

Sophie was quickly concerned after not being able to arouse him. "What's wrong?"

"So much has gone on today and I'm just so tired," he lied.

Reluctantly, Sophie believed he was telling the truth. Being very tired herself, she turned over in bed and fell asleep quickly.

Sophie arose early the next morning to fix breakfast for Carl. The previous night was forgotten; however, it remained filed away in her mind. Carl went off to work and came home as usual. Sophie assumed everything was normal. She was so glad to be home.

One day that week Carl decided they needed an extension telephone in the basement close to his workshop. He told Sophie he was tired of having to run up and down the stairs every time he got a

107

phone call. Sophie thought it was a good idea also, so they called the phone company and had one installed.

Hang up calls like the one Sophie got when she returned from her trip continued. Shortly after the hang up, the phone would ring again, Carl would answer and sure enough, someone would be on the other end. Sophie wasn't stupid; she started to become very suspicious. Every time she would ask Carl who it was, it was always someone from work and he needed to go somewhere. After getting into the car and leaving, about five minutes later Sophie began to notice that Peg would get into her car and leave, too. Shaking her head, Sophie tried to talk herself out of being suspicious of her husband's possible infidelity. She knew he had cheated on her in Arkansas, but deep down inside she believed that Carl loved her and would never leave his family, not now.

He continued to pacify her with excuses, having sex with her only occasionally and never telling Peg of these encounters. He now had two women and the lies and his feelings started to get complicated.

As soon as he arrived home from work, before even reaching the front door, the phone rang. He always raced to be the first to answer it.

"Hello there, Joe. How's it going?"

Sophie started to send the kids out right before Carl came home from work. Looking out the girl's bedroom window that faced the front of the street, she had a bird's eye view of the driveway and Peg's house. She started to see the same scenario everyday. Carl would get a phone call as soon as he got home. Peg's front and back door would be wide open—they lined up directly with each other letting anyone see straight through her living room and out to her back yard. Apparently, Peg was sending her kids out to play, too, and often with Sophie's own children. She watched Peg sit and talk on the phone, hang up, and move to play the piano. Carl would then hang up within seconds after Peg hung up.

Sophie could not believe what was taking place. *It can't be true! He said he would never leave me! Never! My God! ! Please don't let this be happening! I don't think I can take this.*

SOMEDAY A BLESSING

Sophie's survival skills kicked in. She was going to fight for her husband and set in on her plan to prove the affair. The next day, she called the phone company and asked to have a third line put in. She asked the phone installer if he could put a phone in the girl's bedroom, but if he could also hide the phone lines.

"No way, I don't think I could hide the lines. I have to put in a whole new jack," the phone installer said.

Sophie stood by the TV in the living room where their original phone jack was.

"How about there," she said pointing behind the TV, through the wall into the bedroom closet. "Maybe?"

"Yep, I think that will work," he said as he set off to work.

Anticipating the next phone call with her newly-concealed phone line, Sophie lay on her bed pretending to be napping, knowing that Carl was due home from work at any moment. As predicted, Carl drove up and the phone started ringing. Sophie crept ever so quietly into the girl's room and reached under a pile of blankets. She picked up the receiver as her body shook. She tried to tell herself it was just her imagination and it would be just Joe on the other line. Cupped in her hands, she held the phone to her ear only to hear Pegs voice.

"Do you hear that Carl? They're playing our song. Down by the Riverside."

Sophie was horror-struck. *The river, all this time, the river! He was never fishing, never!* She was in a trance when Carl's voice startled her.

"Did you hear that? It sounded like another phone or someone picking one up. Hang on," he said.

Sophie flew out the girls' room light footed and into hers pretending to still be sleeping. Carl walked to the bedroom door and Sophie could feel him staring at her. He then walked out of the room. Sophie heard his steps echoing down the hall and then down the basement stairs. While he was walking downstairs, Sophie had again crept back into the girls' bedroom and held the receiver back to her ear. She heard Carl pick up the phone again.

109

"No, she's asleep. I'll talk later. See you this weekend. I love you."

Sophie never had a phone in her life until now and it had become her worst enemy. Daily, the calls came and with each one she was pulled to pieces listening to their conversations, meeting places, talk of love making. Carl never stopped suspecting someone had to be on the other line. He went downstairs searching for a set of phone lines off the basement phone he had put in. Sophie always acted like she had just come out of the girls' room from cleaning.

It was all making sense to her now…the calls from Carl telling her to stay longer in Poland and that he would send more money if she needed it. He didn't want her back. *I lost him by going to Poland. Poland. It always takes away from me, why?*

One day after one of Carl's so-called colleagues had called needing his assistance, he left and once again, five minutes later, Peg left. This time, however, the telephone rang, a familiar voice on the other end.

"Did you know your husband is with Peg?"

Sophie immediately got sick to her stomach and fell to her knees. "No, no!" she yelled, "It can't be true."

Even though she had seen and been suspicious of certain activities taking place and had heard the two speak of the activities, she never wanted to believe it was true. The secret had been kept within her own family, now that sanctity was broken and others knew.

Who's voice was that? It sounds so familiar, but I can't place it.

Sophie cried hysterically for hours until Carl returned home. He saw that Sophie's eyes were swollen and red from crying and asked her what was wrong. She told him about the phone call. He immediately went into a rage, stomping back and forth through the living room, screaming at the top of his lungs.

"I'll kill 'em! I'll kill 'em! When I find out who it was, I will kill them! I'll take that bitch down to the Missouri river and drown her!" he screamed.

SOMEDAY A BLESSING

Sophie wanted to believe this was a good sign. Maybe a jealous woman was trying to sabotage their marriage by making up lies. Why else would Carl be so upset about this phone call?

The next day was a Saturday. Carl didn't have to go to work and Sophie decided to clean out the car for him. She started cleaning, wiping down the seats, cleaning the dashboard and windows. She opened the glove box and to her astonishment there was a carton of Winston cigarettes. She didn't smoke and though Carl did he didn't smoke Winstons.

Who would these belong to? she wondered.

She knew Peg smoked, but didn't know what brand. She took the carton of cigarettes into the house, holding them out in front of her.

"Who do these belong to?" she asked Carl.

"I bought them for you…I knew how upset you had been lately and I bought them for you. Maybe they will help relax you," he replied without a hitch. "You always wanted to smoke, so I thought I would let you."

Sophie had never smoked or drank in her life. *Why would my husband, who had been so opposed to these habits, want me to start one now?* She couldn't understand it.

Again things were not making sense. Phone calls like clock work everyday, Carl going fishing, never bringing any fish home.

Sophie asked Carl, "Why do you go fishing all the time, Carl, and why did you want to come to Missouri, of all places?"

"I do this to get away," he explained, "I liked it in Arkansas and you're the one that wanted to leave, not me. I wanted to go to school, but you wanted me to get a job instead."

Sophie sat silently as he went on about all the reasons he was unhappy, pointing the finger at her. He made her feel like she was the one at fault. Not understanding his sudden discontentment with his family life, she felt very strongly that someone or something had slithered into her household while she was gone.

Peg had a husband and three children of her own. How could she have found the time and excuses herself to cover this affair up from her own husband and children? Willie must have been easy going or a complete idiot not to have suspected something was wrong. Come to find out, Willie was quite a drinker, and Peg could easily get away.

"Hey, Willie, watch the kids for me. I have to go to the store," Peg would say and Willie would be content to watch TV and drink his beer.

After the two lovers hung up from another phone call, Sophie with her head hung down in complete sadness and despair, returned to her bed. She was crying hysterically.

How could he do this to us? What should I do now? How can I make this right?

Her life had been so perfect for the first time and now it felt like she was back at the "Glass House." This time everyone was throwing stones at it and it was breaking into pieces all around her. She thought of Peg.

She was supposed to be my friend, or so she thought, *She is married, for Christ's sake! What does she want with my husband?*

Now everything Sophie passed off as nothing was turning into something. It made sense. Peg outside every time Carl was. She realized now that Peg smoked Winston cigarettes. Carl hadn't bought those cigarettes for her...they were Pegs! She had sat in her seat in their car. She smoked in their car, she kissed her husband, and she had sex with her husband in their car! Sophie was getting increasingly sick to her stomach at the thought. That's why Peg would leave every time Carl would leave!

I want to kill her! she thought.

Sophie couldn't call anyone to confide in. Her parents and sisters were overseas, and she couldn't tell them her marriage was coming apart at the seams. She had made so many promises to them. She had told them of her great fortune in the U.S. and how she would send them money when she could. She would help them with anything they needed. They were behind the iron curtain and didn't have the opportunities she now had and she felt she could provide her parents and siblings with some finer things in life. That was another dream now over. Without Carl, she couldn't afford to help her family, she couldn't afford herself.

I can't let that bitch ruin my marriage! I have to do something...something.

The days that passed and Sophie couldn't eat. She was already a thin 100 pounds and her weight continued to drop. She decided she didn't want to say anything to Carl about what she knew. She was going to hope this was a brief affair like his others, and that it would soon end and everything would be back to normal. She couldn't even be the one to leave now: going back to Poland after all of this was an impossibility. She was too ashamed. Her days were filled with sorrow and depression. She could not call or write letters to any of her family or friends.

> Beloved Sophie,
> I'm wiring to you a few words, I don't know what is the matter with you that we are not receiving any letters from you. In the beginning, we have received 2 or 3 letters and telephone calls. When you called to let us know of your arrival home and that is all.
> Dearest Sophie, we are sending this letter with a lady from America who is visited our neighborhood, so I am giving her this letter, she will mail it to you from America. When you receive this letter, send the answer to the address on the next page, and that lady will send your letter to us. I am closing these few words and am waiting for your letter, too.
> Many hugs and kisses,
> sister Stasia

Sophie learned years later that Carl, attempting to be discreet about his affair with Peg, would meet her at the river on weekends. He would take their son David, telling Sophie they were going fishing. It would get dark and Carl would tell David to stay on the river banks of the Missouri river and wait for him. David told his mother years later that he was there for hours, it seemed. He hated it and was scared to death, but it made Carl look good leaving home with one of his children, in hopes to throw the neighborhood off.

The neighborhood gossip was running rampant. Sophie's trusted friends, Lonnie Wilson and Donna Smith, kept quiet even though they knew Carl was cheating on Sophie. Lilly continued to make calls to Sophie, trying to disguise her voice.

"Your husband is with Peg," she would say and hang up quickly.

By this time the phone calls were not telling her anything she didn't already know. One phone call was explicit on the whereabouts of Carl and Peg.

"They are at the Green Gables." It was a bar on Highway 24.

Sophie started getting dressed, thinking how she was going to catch them this time. Thoughts raced through her mind about all she was going to say to them. She couldn't wait, but Carl had the car and she didn't feel she should get the neighbors involved. She wondered if this may not be a trap, maybe it was a set up. She would go to the bar and Carl would find her there instead so he could say she was going out on him. He had already accused her of having an affair with some guy named Woody, and had the nerve to accuse her that David was not even his child. She decided not to go, sending her children off to bed early. She sat on the edge of the bed, distraught. Leaning back into bed her mind flooded in thoughts, tears flowed as she tried to keep her eyes dry. She did not want Carl to know she had been crying. She was stronger than that.

I'm a good person, she tried to convince herself, *and I don't deserve this. I don't.*

Everyone in the neighborhood finally thought it was best that Sophie heard about the affair. Neighbors began coming to the house one by one, telling her of their suspicions and what they thought she should do. Sophie thought what was best for her was to keep her mouth shut and hope the bitch went away or that Willie would find out and kill her. Peg and Carl were being confronted by several people as it became everyone's affair. Sophie finally decided there was too much talk about HER life. Maybe everyone else was right and she was wrong. Maybe she needed to confront Carl.

SOMEDAY A BLESSING

That night when Carl came home from work, she did just that.
"I know you're cheating on me with Peg," she said.
"You're crazy. I'm not cheating, and you don't know what the hell you're talking about!" he replied.
Sophie looked at Carl. "What does she do that makes her better than me? I'll do anything you want, just don't leave me and the kids."
Carl looked at Sophie and replied, "No, you're not that kind of woman."
The confrontation continued to escalate to a heated argument. Carl finally grabbed the car keys and headed for the door with Sophie clinging to his arms and legs.
"Carl, Carl, please don't leave...please!"
Carl pulled away from her and slammed the door in her face as he left. He did not come home until the next day. Sophie was exhausted in her torment, and she could hardly hold her head up. It was getting increasingly more difficult to hide everything from the kids as well as take care of them. Deborah had just started kindergarten and Denise was still at home. Sophie found herself depending more and more on Lonnie or Donna to baby sit for her while she tried to salvage what she had left of her marriage.
Peg was not going to back down from this affair. She decided she wanted Carl and she told Willie everything. Willie quickly packed his bags and left without a fight. Peg was glad to see him go. She didn't have to hide anything from him now.
How can I get rid of Sophie, she thought.
Carl finally told Sophie he thought it would be best if he moved out. That sent her even further into a downhill spiral. An argument again broke out, in front of Deborah this time. Deborah watched in horror as Carl dragged Sophie by the arm into the bedroom. She followed and sat down on the bed as she watched her father pulling his clothes out of the closet and her mother begging him to stop.
"Where's Daddy going, Mother?" she asked repeatedly.
Neither Carl nor Sophie heard a word Deborah said. He grabbed what clothes he could and headed out the door with Sophie crying hysterically behind him. Deborah was now crying, too. She was six

years old and had never seen this kind of encounter with her parents before. Sophie turned and hugged Deborah, apologizing to her but unable to explain what had just happened.

Before, when Sophie had been so fed up with her life in Arkansas with Carl and only having one child, it seemed it would have been so much easier to leave him. Now, with four children, a beautiful home, a once beautiful life, she did not want this to end...

Chapter Nine
Vows Broken

Carl had left his home and family in a fit of rage, angered at the fact that this time, he had been caught. Not only that, but this time people were talking. Carl's short, secretive affairs and always being able to return to his content home were over. This time, he found his little game exposed to the world. Carl had found himself in too deep. The woman he chose to be adulterous with was fatally attracted. This was not going to be just an affair as far as Peg was concerned. He was furious that Sophie had been told of his flings with Peg during and after her trip to Poland. He was sure that she was too stupid to think or even suspect that anything was even going on between himself and Peg. Now he needed more time to sort out his feelings, but his card was being forced to be played now. It infuriated him; he had always been the one in control.

The affair was no secret for Peg because she had told some of the other wives. She bragged of them both leaving and coming home just seconds apart of each other, bold and proud they flaunted their works of deception, their only worry was to hide it from Sophie. She was dead-fast in her decision that this was the man she loved and wanted to spend the rest of her life with. Her kids would be fine: they would still have a father, a father that she loved. Carl's four children would just have to pay the price. If they wanted to be with their father, they would have to accept her, something she had thought over well in her mind.

Shortly after leaving, Carl rented a small apartment. Peg visited often with and without her children in the open now. It wasn't long before Peg started encouraging her children to call Carl "Daddy." He would often pick up his children and spend the afternoon at Peg's parent's house. This tore the children to pieces as Peg's kids called out "Dad" when they spoke to Carl. Denise looked up at Peg's daughter Patty in shock when she heard her call Carl dad for the first time. She was so confused. How can these kids, who were once her neighbors, now be calling her father, "Dad?" She felt hurt.

"Why did you leave Mom?" Denise asked her father.

"Things just happen. Go outside and play," her father replied abruptly putting a stop to the subject.

Sophie was alone now, going through the motions like a robot on autopilot. She fixed breakfast for the children, got them off to school and then spent the rest of the day crying, uncontrollably at times. Her weight continued to drop. The very thought of Peg having her husband made her terribly ill. She picked up the telephone receiver and slowly dialed the number to Peg's parents' home. Sophie knew where Peg's parents lived and was able to locate their number in the phone book. When Peg's mother answered the phone, Sophie quietly and nervously spoke.

"This is Sophie. I just want to know if you are aware that your daughter Peg is breaking up my marriage."

"If you don't know how to keep your man, that's your problem," Peg's mother replied sarcastically. Sophie was a loss for words.

Sophie's mind raced with memories. At that moment, Sophie remembered she had once heard through the grapevine that Peg's mother herself had been involved in an adulterous affair and had broken up a marriage to steal a Pharmacist from his wife and children.

"Like mother like daughter!" Sophie yelled into the receiver and slammed the phone down.

SOMEDAY A BLESSING

As Carl continued his visits with his children, it seemed they were always spending their time at Peg's parents' house. They began to see less and less of Carl as Peg pushed all the kids outside to play. Occasionally, she would gather all the children together only for pictures with their new brothers and sister, and their new mom, Peg. Daryl and David were older and struggled with their feelings when the two other boys who used to be their neighbors were now calling their father "Dad" and wrestling around with him in the yard. The competition became fierce between the siblings. Carl's children became insecure in sharing their dad and Peg encouraged the kids to call her mom. None of the kids did, EVER! There was never any doubt that Carl wanted them all to be one big happy family and leave Sophie completely out. Peg, however, never had any intentions of it happening. Only if indeed it left Sophie alone and devastated would she even consider putting up with Carl's kids. She was really in a dilemma. She had to keep Carl happy and Sophie miserable. If anyone was going to pay a price in this divorce, it was going to be anyone but her.

Each time Carl and Peg picked up the kids, Sophie worried it would be the last time she would ever see them. She thought that since Carl and Peg were dead-set in destroying her life anyway, what would stop them from trying to take her children, too? She even started to fear for her life. Carl became so angry at the courts, what would stop him from attempting to just get rid of her? Standing at the door waving goodbye to the kids as Carl sped off, never once did she think that she needed to start a life of her own. She was so tired of starting over and over again, only to have war and now love lost take it all away from her.

She now found her world spinning out of control. All the promises she had made to her family back in Poland were not possible to keep now. The final blow was the letter she received from her Uncle Franciszik, who had been shot and imprisoned during the war where he contracted Tuberculosis. Sophie and Carl had been sending him Penicillin secretly through the iron curtain disguising the much needed medicine as Christmas Presents.

119

How do I tell him I'm so sorry, she thought as she opened the letter.

Dear Sophie and your entire family,
I'm sending you loving greetings and thoughtfulness. I promised you, beloved, to write and let you know of my improvement or the lack of it, with the medicine which you, my beloved, have sent to me. The improvement is very great, the lungs are responding very well and is hope for complete healing.
There is the need of at least two more bottles of the same medicine and the same size of bottles, request of the doctors. It is impossible for me to buy the medicine here, beloved Sophie, I don't have the courage to appeal to you that you should send me two more. I am thinking of the cost involved, but for the time being, I can not repay you. All I can do for now is lovingly thanking you. Maybe you will come to beloved Poland like you wrote your Mommy and then maybe I will be able to repay you.
Sophie, I will close for now, and I am sorry for any hardships this may have caused you and your family.
Hugs,
Your Uncle Franciszik

Many other letters left unopened on the coffee table, she could not bring herself to read any more. She could not find the words to write back to tell them she could no longer help, she was now the one in need of help. All the letters she saved but never answered, they would only be brought out years later on occasions when she would sit at the dinner table, drinking the night away. Pictures scattered out with bundles of letters begging for an answer from her. Pen and paper in hand, empty were the pages only stained with her tears. Alone, even with all the languages she now knew, still there were no words to fill the lines. She felt she had caused them all too many worries and

SOMEDAY A BLESSING

pain, and her children she would now face. No words, no excuses, it was time for her to leave…

Sophie asked Lonnie if she would watch the kids for a couple of hours. She quietly went into her bedroom, sat on the bed and stared off into the walls that were once occupied with the one that she loved.

She heard the faint laughter of her children echoing down the hallway as she drifted off into a sea of memories raging against her mind. Over and over the voices of Nazi's yelling; visions of Jews being marched down the snow-blanketed streets with no shoes; Carl and Peg's conversations on the phone; her children's cries, "Why did dad leave us?"

Slowly, she picked up two bottles of over-the-counter sleeping pills she had purchased earlier that day. Sophie had finally come to the conclusion that even though she loved her children and Carl with all her heart and soul, she could not take the pain any longer. She couldn't live with the thought of her family back in Poland finding out or thinking she was a failure. She could not live without Carl, the only man she would ever love. She didn't want to have her children raised in a single parent home. One at a time, she swallowed all of the pills. As each one touched her tongue, she wept even harder. The thoughts that ran through her mind were too well known. It was not the first time she wanted to end her life, and when she came across the ocean with Carl, she was glad she had not. She just knew that this was what her life would be all about: having a family, helping her parents, and being in love.

She lay down on the bed and cried softly as she succumbed to the slumber the pills eventually inflicted. Drifting off into her first restful sleep, her eyes became heavy for the first time in months. Feelings of complete rest and peace brought a chill to her bones, but her mind would not sleep. She had visions of family, God, war planes raging down on her, soldiers' feet pounding the ground behind her, guns in her face, glass and buildings crashing with explosive waves of sound. Tighter and tighter she closed her eyes, still seeing the remembrances of her past life. She then saw a vision of her mother standing at the window; a tear fell from her mother's eyes, rolling down her cheek.

What are you doing Sophie? Where are you? I can't come get you if I don't know where you are, Sophie!

Sophie cried out weakly, "Mother, I'm far from home and I can't sleep. Mother, I can't sleep, save me! Save me! Mother please...please come get me..."

Lonnie became worried when Sophie had not come over to pick up her children. She went next door and knocked, no answer, she knocked harder. Still no answer. Lonnie went back next door and got her husband, "I can't get Sophie to answer the door," she told him, "and her car is in the driveway. I know she has to be home. I'm worried."

Chuck called the police and hurriedly explained the situation. They arrived shortly thereafter and made entrance into the Raney home. Sophie lied curled up in bed, the pillows wet with tears. She was barely responsive and the empty sleeping pill bottles lay on the floor next to her bed. The police called on their radio to send an ambulance immediately.

"She's still breathing and she has a pulse," they reported.

Rushing Sophie to the Independence Sanitarium, her stomach was pumped of the many pill fragments left. She was admitted to Intensive Care for observation and an attempt to save her life. The children remained with Lonnie and Chuck until they could locate Carl.

Lonnie got a hold of Lilly. She knew that Lilly was still in close contact with Peg and that she would know how to get Carl's phone number. She was right, shortly after telling Lilly Sophie was in Intensive Care for an attempted suicide, Carl called Lonnie.

"How is she? Is she okay? Is she going to live?" he seemed concerned.

Lonnie told Carl that it was still touch and go according to hospital personnel but they thought she would most likely make it.

Carl asked Lonnie if she could keep the kids overnight and he headed for the hospital. When he entered the ICU, he saw Sophie

SOMEDAY A BLESSING

lying in a hospital bed, curled into a fetal position. She looked so small, so frail and for a fleeting moment, he felt sorry for her. He wanted to comfort her and hold her. The only thing stopping him was Peg. He knew that Peg would be livid when she even found out he was even at the hospital. Carl woke Sophie and told her that her kids needed her, that she couldn't kill herself. He said she needed to stay strong for the children. Sophie cried as she looked up at the man that held all her hopes and dreams in the palm of his hands. He was asking her to keep going for the children? He never mentioned that he would come back to her, that he would make things right again, that he realized how much she and his family meant to him.

Sophie had achieved one thing from her attempt on her life. She had Carl worried about her. She had him at the hospital next to her, even though it was only for a brief moment; he was there and was there for the four children they shared.

Returning home, she was welcomed by some of the neighbors and her children. Donna Smith and her husband Bud had befriended Sophie, telling her if there was anything she needed to let them know. She soon realized that Carl's interest in her after the attempt on her life was short lived. He returned to his apartment and continued seeing Peg. It was over this time for sure, there was nothing else she could do to get him back. She needed to concentrate on her kids and getting work to support them.

The phone rang. It was Grandpa Jeff, telling Sophie to hire an attorney.

"You had better get a lawyer before he does. You need support for yourself and those kids," he told her.

Sophie contacted James Titus, who would become a Jackson County Judge in his future years. Mr. Titus was a well-respected attorney in the Independence area. When he met Sophie for the first time, he was very reassuring to her.

"Your husband has a good job, Sophie. He will have to pay child support and alimony to you." Titus soon drew up the legal documents to proceed with the separation and eventual dissolution of the

123

marriage. Titus had an order for temporary support granted through the court.

Sophie had so many people telling her what to do next, she was simply following commands by this point. She didn't want a divorce: she wanted her family back, intact.

When Carl was served with papers for legal separation, he was both distressed and angry. He had the best of both worlds. He had his children, and he had Peg and his own apartment where he could still act like a single man. Now he was faced with money issues. Carl was already spending a lot of money on his apartment and on Peg and her children. Now he was going to have to pay Sophie. As long as there were no lawyers involved, he could spend his money when and on whom he wanted.

Carl called Peg and told her about the papers.

"Well, you need to get divorced from her so we can go on with our lives! We can try to get the children if you want, Carl. I will stand by you no matter what you decide. I love you and want to be with you always. You need to leave this old life behind you! You told me yourself she only wanted a free ticket to the States! Well, she's here now; you owe her nothing. Let her family help her! God knows you've helped them!"

The court orders demanded child support and temporary alimony until the final divorce. Carl was also ordered to pay on all the creditors for their furniture, car, and boat. He was having to support two families now, since Peg had driven her husband off and immediately filed for divorce, asking for nothing from him except to get out of she and her kids' life. Both Sophie and Peg had no income, and Carl now had seven kids to care for now. Peg played on Carl's financial obligations, convincing him that Sophie was an evil person, that she was only out for one thing and that was MONEY!

Carl started sending checks to Sophie via a neighbor that worked with him. In one of the envelopes Carl had a note attached.

HERE IS SOME MORE BLOOD MONEY. I SENT SOME TO YOUR LAWYER. WILL SEND MORE AS SOON AS POSSIBLE!

SOMEDAY A BLESSING

Peg had Carl believing that Sophie was spending every dime on herself. She had even stooped so low as to have Lilly lie to Carl and tell him that Denise, who was five at the time, was going door to door begging for food because Sophie was not feeding her children. The divorce was near completion and the court date was coming up soon. What a big surprise: Peg was pregnant with her and Carl's child. Peg was ecstatic as she had finally got her man and now their love child. It was all in her plan. Peg thought it would be so much easier for Carl to leave his four children if he had a child of his own with her. She privately prayed for a son. Sophie felt the worst was over; maybe they would leave her alone now so she could just care for her children.

Carl's sister Margaret called Sophie, pretending to be so concerned about all she must have gone through. Carl and Sophie spent a lot of time with Margaret and her husband Raymond. Raymond was quite the fisherman, too. Carl and he would share the love of water, boating and fishing with both their families. Sophie had always felt she could trust Marge.

"You ought to get away with the kids for a few days before the divorce is final," Marge said. "Why don't you take the kids and go down to Grandpa Jeff's for a few days? It will help you to get a little time away from all this crap."

Sophie reluctantly agreed. Marge, after all, had always seemed to be on Sophie's side and had seemingly only wanted what was best for her. When Sophie had once asked Margaret why Carl would even leave her for Peg, Margaret is the one that told Sophie "Because she sucks his dick. She's a slut, Sophie."

Sophie called Grandpa Jeff and told him she and the kids were coming for a visit. Grandpa Jeff told her to be sure to lock up the house and be careful on the drive down.

"Call me if you have any car trouble or anything, I'll come get you," he said.

He was delighted at the thought of seeing his grandchildren, but wary of Sophie leaving the house. He knew his son all too well.

125

Unbeknownst to Sophie, Margaret had been instructed by Carl and Peg to get Sophie out of town.

"She still trusts you, Margaret, you're the only one we know that can get her out of that house for a few days," Carl said.

While Sophie was gone, Carl proceeded to carry out his plan. He busted in the basement door and started loading up everything he wanted out of the house. He hooked up the speed boat and away he went. Everything of value was taken. Sophie returned to see that the basement and front doors had been broken into. She immediately knew who it was and she knew who had forsaken her, Margaret.

Who can I trust now? she thought.

Denise, who was only five at the time, heard her mother come into the living room. "He even took the rolls of quarters I had saved."

Sophie called her attorney the next day and told him what had happened while she was out of town. Titus told Sophie not to worry; that she would get her essentials back in the divorce and that Carl could not legally take those things. He said everything had to be accounted for and divided in the upcoming court proceedings.

Dona Smith knocked on Sophie's door after hearing the rumors of Carl breaking into her house. "You better hide your car; he will come and get that, too," Dona told Sophie.

Sophie parked the car in Bud and Dona's garage two houses down. One evening she forgot, and the very next morning the car was gone. She could not believe it.

Someone here in the neighborhood has to be watching me, she thought.

She didn't know who to trust now, who was watching her, and what was going to happen next. She understood the boat; she wouldn't use it anyway, but the car?

I can't believe he took the car! How do I get to work, go to the store, or take the children to the Doctor?

The divorce finally took place. The household items that Carl took were to be returned to Sophie. In the divorce decree, Sophie was granted the house, child support, alimony, and Carl was ordered to return the car. Sophie began to think that maybe she could make it.

SOMEDAY A BLESSING

With some financial support from her now ex-husband, she could maybe take a part-time job and still be there for her children.

March 3, 1961
Dear Grandma:

How are you and Elsie? Wish we could come down and see you, or if you were more able I sure would like to have you stay with me and the boys & girls. Well, it's all over between me and Carl. He has gotten his divorce that he wanted so bad. I feel like I am all alone in this world, but I have faith that God will help me to raise these kids and keep them together. I am trying to go to work, but it's so hard to find one that would allow me to be here in the morning to send them off to school and be back when they come back from school.

Next fall I might get a job at the school cafeteria. The boys and Debra have been going to school everyday. They are getting free lunches at school. People sure have been nice to me.

I wish I had my mother over here. She sure would be a lot of help to me. Maybe when I go to work, and I can save some money to get her or my dad over here.

I will close and hope to see you soon.

Sophie & children

Shortly after the divorce was final, Peg and Carl got married at the courthouse. Sophie knew they were getting married because she received a bill for a wedding ring set from Goldman's Jewelers sent to her address. Carl was still putting things on their joint credit cards and using his old address. Peg and Carl had a few friends at their courthouse wedding and afterwards drove around the streets of Independence with "JUST MARRIED" sprayed on the convertible they had borrowed.

Peg told Carl, "Let's drive down Pearl Street. We still have friends there and they would want to see us."

Acting like two teenagers, they did just that, with no thought of the wounds they would inflict on four little kids that day.

Sophie was just finishing up the dinner dishes as the kids sat around the television. In a far off distance, car horns were blowing, louder and louder as they came around the corner onto Pearl.

"Someone got married," Daryl said.

They all ran out to see who it was, but Sophie stayed inside. Everyone wondered who they knew that would be getting married. The honking vehicles raced into the neighborhood as the kids quickly ran outside to see what the commotion was all about. The four Raney kids stood in the middle of the yard as Daryl held his arms out to stop the other three from going any farther. Nothing was said between them as they stood watching their father with his new bride, honking and waving. The happy couple drove past Sophie's house. Peg dressed in off-white, smiling widely as she watched Sophie peeking through the window, waving precociously to the children. The children watched in dismay as their father drove off with another woman. Peg had the look of a winning marathon racer on her face as they quickly disappeared around the corner. Daryl slowly walked back into the house, and looked at his mother sadly.

"It was Dad, Mom. It was Dad and Peg."

Daryl was only 11 years old, but he was old enough to know that what just happened was done only to hurt his mother. All the children gathered around Sophie hoping to make her feel better, but they also were torn up inside themselves. Carl and Peg probably will never know how they destroyed four children's lives on that day. They had taken material things and now they took their hearts, scarring them forever.

The child support and alimony checks continued to come to Sophie for a short time after the divorce via a neighbor. However, this time the checks were made out by Peg and made payable to Sophie Stanski, signed by Peg Raney. Peg was thrilled to rub it in Sophie's face by signing Raney as her last name. She had complete control of Carl, she was pregnant with his child, and he was now her husband. Now she needed to get Carl away, away from "that family."

SOMEDAY A BLESSING

Carl and Peg soon decided if they moved out of state, they could keep everything he had stolen from Sophie's house and they wouldn't have to pay her another dime. They soon packed up and moved to Minnesota. Carl had talked Ford Motor Company into giving him a transfer to the Minneapolis plant. Sophie's attorney continued to track Carl down and located him through the employment. It was the mid-1960s, and child support enforcement was nonexistent. It was easy to be a deadbeat dad and never have to support your children. Titus sent Carl certified letters demanding that he pay the money owed Sophie and his children, and to return her stolen belongings. Carl refused to respond to these demands.

"You'd be better off if he was dead. At least you would get his Social Security for the children," Grandpa Jeff told Sophie.

Peg enrolled her children in school using "Raney" as their last names. Their love child was born and they named him a biblical name, "Jacob." They bought a nice home and started out on their journey to find peace of mind.

Carl sent Sophie less money and less often. Titus' hands were tied since Carl lived in another state. It was getting more and more difficult to force Carl to pay.

He was happy with Peg, Jacob, and Peg's children in their new home. He wanted to have his children with him, that way Sophie would be alone and on her own. He would have his kids and not have to send her another dime, ever. Peg didn't like this idea one bit, but she agreed that maybe the kids could come to visit for a few weeks, a trial period. She knew she needed to keep Carl happy and appease him in any way she could. He would always tell his kids when they were older how Peg stood by him through the big ordeal of his divorce and how Sophie drained him of all his money.

Sophie had been working at the Coffee Shop on Highway 24 as a waitress part-time after Carl left her. She had to pay cab fare to and from work since she was left without a vehicle and no means to purchase another. When Deborah fell and cut her chin requiring stitches, Sophie had to have Lonnie take her to the doctor for the emergency. Lonnie also babysat for Sophie and occasionally

129

brought the children to the shop for hot fudge sundaes and to see their mother. On Sunday afternoons, Sophie watched as families came to the Coffee Shop after church. It killed her to see families so happy together. She had to excuse herself and go to the bathroom to cry before returning to her job and forcing a happy face for her patrons. *I should be able to be home with my children,* she thought.

Deborah missed her mother terribly. She called the restaurant several times a day and when Sophie got on the line, Deborah would be crying.

"I want you to come home."

"I'll be home soon honey, I promise," Sophie told her.

She found a neighborhood teen who could baby-sit and paid her to sit with the kids in the evenings that she worked. Soon that was a luxury she could no longer afford. When Daryl was twelve, he became the babysitter/father of the family.

Carl called Sophie and asked if he could pick up the children and keep them for the summer. Carl had already been enticing the children to come to Minnesota and Peg had even followed up with a letter after they had a short visit with their dad.

> Dearest Daryl,
>
> How is that growing boy? You certainly look wonderful and just like your father. I never saw such a likeness. Your dad is real happy that he saw you all and is very proud of you. I am proud of you, too, and think every one of you children are well-behaved and darling. Be sure and tell David, Deborah, and Denise that we send them our love and that we were very happy to have seen them, even if it wasn't as long as we would have liked.
>
> Daryl, you are all invited up here. We love all of you and really enjoy all of you. We have to make the arrangements and it will probably have to be just two at a time because of the trip involved. What we would really like is to have all four of you all the time. I think the 10 of

SOMEDAY A BLESSING

us make a nice family, (just think what a ball team we would have, ha).

We are taking a trip to Canada in August and hope you are here to go with us, David, too, of course.

We left the next evening after seeing you all. The trip home was nice and we arrived early the next morning. The garden had really grown and surprised me. Daddy has built a cute fence and designed a trellis so we painted that yesterday. It matches the house. We nearly croaked in that hot weather down there and we have had lots of rain since we got home, but at least it isn't real hot. It is very cool in the summer here.

Remember your dad telling you about the Minnesota River? We went down there fishing last Friday night and that was fun.

Your dad said to tell you he had been longing to see you children and is so happy that he got to. He thinks you are all real good looking and just as good as can be. That Denise is as smart as she can be, too. I thought she said the cutest things. I hope she still has her bracelet.

I hope your sunburn is better. I know you were uncomfortable that day. I am doing some sunning now and getting more tan. Your dad likes for me to get real tanned.

Take real good care of yourself and those swell brother and sisters. We all send a big hello and all our love,

Peg

Sophie knew she would miss her kids, but with bills now mounting beyond her control, it would give her a chance to find a better job and get caught up.

Carl, with of course Peg attached to his hip, arrived for the kids about a week later. Sophie kissed them all goodbye, fearing that it would be the last time she would ever see them. The children, excited about a trip to another state and being able to see their dad again, ran to the car excitedly. Piling in, Carl and Peg drove off without a wave and headed back to Minnesota. Carl soon had his boys and girls convinced of a better life with him. This great life he convinced the kids they would have, came with a price.

"You can come live with us permanently, but you will have to get along with Peg."

Peg was becoming the epitome of a "wicked stepmother."

Carl called Sophie and told her that the kids wanted to stay Minnesota with him. He told Sophie they would be down to pick up the kids belongings soon. Sophie was devastated.

He did it, he left me and now he is taking my children.

During the time the children were gone, Sophie found a better job at the Holiday Inn restaurant at Highway 40 and Noland Road. It was further from her house, but the clientele paid better tips there and she planned on providing for herself and her children. She had also taken side jobs cleaning houses and ironing clothes for extra cash. While at work one night, a large coffee urn exploded as she walked past it. The scalding hot coffee blew onto Sophie's hip and leg causing 1st, 2nd and 3rd degree burns. She was taken to the hospital where her wounds were treated in the ER. She was unable to go to work until her burns healed; however, she continued to iron clothes for people. She had to keep making money.

Carl and Peg arrived at the front of Sophie's house with the children. They were there to pick up the kids' clothing and toys for the move to Minnesota. The kids went into the house where they saw their mother with gauze dressings covering her entire left leg and hip. Sophie was standing at the ironing board. She put the iron down and reached for her children, all of them hugging her, careful not to touch her wounds.

"What happened?" they asked.

Sophie explained the accident to the children. All four of her kids were distraught at seeing the suffering their mother was going through, all alone.

The kids told their mom that they liked it at their dad's, but they hated Peg. Sophie told them they needed to make a decision.

SOMEDAY A BLESSING

"I don't want you to go," she stated, "but your dad is waiting for you. You all need to decide what you want to do."

Deborah and Denise started to cry. They couldn't leave their mother. Not now...she needed them. Daryl and David felt the same way, but their feelings came without tears.

"We don't want to leave, we want to stay here," David said.

Deborah, David, and Denise were terrified at the thought of telling their dad they had changed their minds. Daryl had basically become the man of the house.

"I'll go tell them," he offered.

Daryl walked slowly out to the car where Carl and Peg waited.

"We're not going, Dad. We changed our minds."

"What?" Carl said, "I thought you kids wanted to be with me!"

"Mom's hurt," Daryl replied. "We can't leave her right now."

Peg gave Daryl a hateful look, a look he had become all too familiar with.

"I hope you are happy at what you are doing to your father!" she yelled.

Carl stomped on the gas and peeled out in the gravel shooting gravel back at Daryl as they sped away.

Daryl returned to the house where the other three children had been watching out the window. The kids were both scared and confused. Why would their father not want his children to be happy? Why would he be so mad at them? Any future contact with their dad would be scarce, mainly through letters, often times written by Peg bragging of what a great life they were having.

Chapter Ten
The Search for Peace

Carl and Peg returned to Minnesota. The entire trip home, Peg filled Carl's head with thoughts of how low it was of his own children and how they couldn't possibly love him. If so, they would have come home with him.

"I can't believe he just stood there and told you they were staying with her!" Peg said smugly, "After all you've done for them."

Peg hurt for Carl, but in her own devious way, she was glad the kids were not coming back with them. Peg had made their lives miserable while living with them. They were never so happy to see their dad coming home from work so Peg would get off their asses.

Peg screamed at Carl the moment he drove up from work and got him cornered in the bedroom while she filled him in on the day's catastrophic events. The end result was always the same: one of the four taking a trip down to the basement for a whipping. Surely her own kids felt a bit of relief knowing Carl's children were there to take the bulk of all Peg's hateful tendencies toward all the children.

Everyone believed she would have given up her own children in order to have Carl all to herself, but she needed them as a replacement to cushion the blow of Carl having to give up his own. The lesser of the two evils, she picked her own kids, as they swiftly changed their names to Raney.

134

SOMEDAY A BLESSING

Carl battled his own demons and anger he held against his own father for splitting up him and his sister Margaret after his parents divorced. Peg never stopped trying to do drive a wedge between Carl and his kids. He never knew all the scandalous ways about her, her backstabbing and trickery. She was good at it, but a person had to be blind not to see it. Daryl, David, Deborah, and Denise certainly saw it.

Peg would be laughing one moment and running around the next in frenzy, acting like it was all just too much for her. Her personality changed like the weather. It could never be forecasted with accuracy. She would decide what the weather was going to be every day and only when it would make Carl happy did the sun shine.

One weekend Carl took the family on a hunting trip, wanting to teach the boys to shoot. He didn't want Jacob or Denise around the guns, so Patty volunteered to stay at the car and watch them. Peg followed Carl and the boys close behind before disappearing over the hill. She looked back and reminded Patty to keep the baby Jacob off the car; he was about three at the time.

How funny, Denise thought, *he is such a brat anyway and he's not stupid, either.*

Sure enough, the minute they were out of sight, up on the car he went. Jacob began jumping up and down on the hood. Denise was ready to grab the little brat and shake him to death.

"NO! We'll get in to trouble," Patty scolded her for her reaction.

In trouble? Denise thought. She could not believe the fear she saw in Patty's eyes. She was really scared to death to touch or scold him.

For an hour they watched him dance about on the car, sticking his tongue out, knowing all the while his ass was covered. It would be Denise and Patty who paid dearly for his intentional damaging conduct. When the family returned, Peg saw Jacob stomping around on the car. She immediately flew into a rage, focused on Denise and Patty. Jacob had purposely disobeyed his mother, but he was never to blame.

"Do you see this Carl?! See what they let Jacob do to your car? I can't believe it! They were supposed to watch him and now look what they let him do!"

Denise and Patty knew all too well that it was inevitable they would be in big trouble as they sat on the ground, feeling nonexistent. Peg continued on her malicious rampage.

Denise attempted several times to interject her defense only finding her statements ignored and stomped on by Peg's frenzy. She finally just flipped her the finger, sure that Peg had not seen her. Patty, however, did see her. Patty thought this was a great opportunity to get some of the slack off her, and was set to tell her mother about Denise's obscene gesture. Sure enough, by the time they got home, down the basement Denise went for another whipping.

"You know I don't want to do this," Carl told Denise.

"Then why are you?" she asked.

"Because I have to."

At eight years old, she did not understand that kind of thinking, but she knew two wrongs don't make a right. Denise accepted her punishment, but kept an eye on the one that had a lot more in store for this family of four trying to come in between them.

All the kids enjoyed torturing Jacob about his baby blanket. It was no doubt his life line, as they ran around the house hiding it from him. Denise threw it in the bathtub, not realizing someone had just finished taking a bath and the tub was still wet. It turned out to be the end of the world for Jacob and Peg. Peg had to put the sacred blanket in the dryer, while Jacob screamed the entire time it was locked up in the tumbling dungeon. The kids were all punished and the Raney kids soon realized the hard way they need to stay out of the house and away from the evil one. Nothing done meant nothing said, by Peg. Staying out of the house for hours soon took its toll on the Raney kids. Torn between Carl and Sophie, they began to really miss their own rooms and their mother. They loved their dad but felt it was not worth all the over-exaggeration and deceit going on between them and Peg.

SOMEDAY A BLESSING

Carl and Peg had many arguments through the years about his children. Peg thought of ways to be inconspicuous. She never allowed Carl to answer the phone. If Sophie needed to talk to him or one of the kids wanted to call him, she made sure that every call had to be filtered through her first. Carl's children were never again allowed to talk to their father without Peg grilling them first about what they wanted. Often times, Peg told them he was not home and would never tell Carl they had even called. He wrote letters to his children and stuffed the envelope full of pictures, their boating, ski trips, 4-wheelers, deep sea fishing, and camping. Peg made sure she was in every one of the pictures sent. This would continue on into the children's teen years.

"See what you missed." It was written all over her face.

The bragging went on about Peg's kids and Jacob and talking about how much fun the kids were having. They started a band, a TV show, etc. Their seemingly pleasant letters filled with details of their everyday lives seemed to fulfill their own purpose to intentionally make the Raney children regret their choice to stay with their mother.

The kids wrote their father letters, but only at Peg's discretion would they be given to him. The others were destroyed by Peg before Carl got home from work.

Carl soon began to believe that Peg was right. His kids didn't care about him.

"What will be will be." He wasn't going to fight it anymore.

Carl had a spiritual side to him and wanted to explore that realm. Basically, he needed to find a way to forgive himself for the destruction he had left behind in Independence. He knew that his own father, Grandpa Jeff, was extremely disappointed in Carl for leaving Sophie and his own children, reliving his own mistakes, and he knew that his father hated Peg. His guilt began to eat him up inside.

Carl and Peg soon started calling around to different churches inquiring about their biblical beliefs. Several people from different denominations would visit their home and study the Bible with them.

137

He soon was able to spout out scripture; he was beginning to like this Bible thing. He and Peg started to attend church, but there was only one hitch. Every church they attended taught the same thing. "Thou shall not commit adultery." That commandment was like a hot poker stabbing into Carl's heart. He knew deep down inside that no matter how spiritual he became, the right thing to do in the eyes of God was to support his children and that he had broken a commandment and committed "adultery."

Carl had a war going on in his mind; he needed to do the right thing, but how?

One night, Peg told Carl that she had some visitors at the door earlier in the day. She had invited them to come back to house after Carl got home from work.

"They called themselves Jehovah's Witnesses," she told him. "Might be a good idea to hear what they have to say."

She already knew the struggle Carl was having with what he had left behind. She so wanted to find a way to give Carl peace of mind, a way to make him content with his new family.

That night the Jehovah's Witnesses arrived at the home. They were very friendly people. They sat down at the dining room table with the couple and began to explain their beliefs. They brought along with them the JW Bible along with some *Watchtower* magazines. The *Watchtower* was the JW's monthly publication of Bible teachings.

Carl and Peg were pleased with their new friends and their teachings and decided to start attending their Kingdom Hall. They were soon holding Bible studies at their home. This is when Carl decided to come clean with his new found teachers. He felt by this time that he was close enough to them that he could tell them about his "other" family.

Carl explained to the JWs that he was divorced and had children from a previous marriage. The JWs asked him if his ex-wife and/or children were JWs. He said no and explained that Sophie was Catholic and that his children were raised as Baptists.

SOMEDAY A BLESSING

"Since your children and your ex-wife are not members of the JWs, they are basically lost souls. Jehovah only recognizes those people who believe in our teachings, they will never be allowed into his kingdom."

That was music to Carl's ears, he had finally found a religion that accepted him "as is," so to speak, with all of his past sins. Though the Jehovah's Witnesses disapproved of his divorce, their immediate response was that Carl's duty now was to convert his children to the JW faith to save their souls. That would be the greatest gift he could give to them now. Peg was quite pleased herself. She was happy that Carl could now legitimately forget about his biological children, certain that with all the miles between them they would never convert.

All communications turned into *Watchtower* magazines and the preaching of Jehovah God. As they dug deeper into the new JW religion, Carl became even more convinced that it was not money his kids needed, not even a father image in their lives. He really believed that if he could save their souls, they would thank him in the end for converting them to his new found religion, even though the children resisted and never did convert.

Carl and Peg delved into the church. Before too long, Carl was an elder in the church. He no longer sent his biological children birthday cards or presents because the JWs believed that all holiday's and birthdays were Pagan celebrations. How nice...he didn't even have to remember his other family ever, not ever.

Deborah received a birthday present from her father delivered to her by a taxi driver. It was a box of Russell Stover candy. She had no idea this would be the last present she would ever receive from her father.

Carl continued to be hounded for child support and alimony payments. He and Peg therefore made a decision. They sold everything they owned, purchased a small yacht, and lived on the west coast seas. For the next five years, they cruised with Peg's children and Jacob from port to port, working small jobs to support themselves and never paid another dime to Sophie or his children, with Jehovah's blessings.

Before setting sail, the Raney children received a letter that would be the last time they heard from their father for next five years.

Dear Daryl, David, Deborah, and Denise,
I hope this letter finds you well.

I want to take this opportunity to write one more time and express my thoughts and feelings to you. I know you have been through a lot of emotional upset since October but a lot of that has been out of my hands. I did what I thought was best for you all. Just remember the easiest road is not always the right one.

It has always been my desire that you be given a choice of whom to live with and where to live. Now you have made your choice, right or wrong, and I hope the best for you all. I have always tried not to cause any upsets for you by bothering you and creating an emotional disturbance. So now that you have made this choice, as much as I would like to see you, I will try to make the visits and communications less frequent so as to give you a chance to adjust fully to your new life. I hope that someday you mother will get married and give you a father so that you can have a man around the house. Maybe Johnny will marry your mother and move in entirely.

I know that I have lost respect from you children because your mother has led you to believe that I am being made to send the money to you and to care for you little. As I have stated in the past, I do not have to send the money to you and as I believe money has nothing to do with making you have good or bad morals or makes a better person out of you. As a matter of fact, I have seen many children that have had to work a lot younger than you are and who have grown up to make a better contribution, be better citizens, and be morally upright because they had no one to give them money and the luxuries of life. In other words, money

SOMEDAY A BLESSING

doesn't make a person. I think I would be doing you a favor if I didn't send you any money at all because I don't believe it contributes anything to your family life there or provides a wholesome way of life.

To sum it up, what I am trying to tell you is money is not the most important thing in life. Especially money that isn't earned by you. I have a feeling that too much importance is put on getting easy money there at that house.

My sincere wish is that the decision that you made will bring you endless happiness. Remember you always have a home with me at any time but the next time you come your choice must be here permanently and the custody papers signed over before you come. Just remember you can contact us through Peg's mother and dad in case of emergency.

As I cannot trust your mother in any case at all, there will be no verbal agreements at all—only signed papers. So if you are not sure, make sure that your mother signs the legal papers before you come.

Go to church, remember God, always tell the truth, don't think bad things, and always be good. I wish a world full of happiness for you.

Lots of Love,
your dad

P.S. We will bring the rest of your stuff soon.

Chapter Eleven
Never Stop Dancing

Carl and Peg hit the high seas, running from bills and Sophie. It was early 1964 and all monies ordered by the courts for Carl to pay had long since ceased. Sophie still owed her attorney money he had charged her for the divorce and collection of child support. Sophie continued to work hard, but it was not sufficient enough income to pay the mortgage, utilities, and all the creditors Carl had left unpaid. Paying only bits and pieces of the bills owed only delayed the inevitable. It seemed totally hopeless to her now. Grandpa Jeff, not knowing exactly how bad things were getting, would not hear from Sophie again until the mortgage company threatened and pursued the foreclosure on the house.

A knock at the door brought Sophie to look out the window where she saw a Sheriff with several laborers and two men dressed in suits who seemed to be in charge of what was about to take place. She knew what they were there for. They were there to repossess all the furnishings in her home, the furnishings she and Carl had purchased on credit and used as collateral. Opening the door, she backed up into the living room as the men forced their way in where they served her papers demanding payment. She stood in shock.

"I don't have it," she said sadly.

SOMEDAY A BLESSING

"Well, we have to take everything back then, Mrs. Raney," one of the men replied abruptly.

Neighborhood kids surrounded the truck outside on the street as Daryl walked up.

"Hey, Daryl. What's going on? Are you guys moving?" they asked.

Daryl replied sadly, "No, I don't think so." He knew what was happening.

Sophie's other three kids were playing at the Smiths' house but came running home when they saw all the commotion going on. Running into the house, they saw their mother standing in the middle of the living room. They could tell she was trying to fight back tears. They walked up to her, laying their hands on her arms. Not a word was spoken as they watched the men pulling plugs out of the wall sockets. They tossed pictures and figurines on the floor, dollies loaded up the refrigerator and stove, banging them against the door frames as a line of the furnishings trailed out the front door toward the awaiting truck. The family of five stood seemingly unnoticed while the workers continued to load up their lives. The men continued, taking the sofa, chairs, end tables, and lamps.

"Anything else, boss?" One asked.

"Yeah, the bedroom furniture down the hall. There are three bedroom sets and don't forget the television."

Sophie asked her children to go next door and wait, knowing that by then they had seen way too much. With her children reluctantly leaving their mother's side, they filed out the front door as she assured them with a smile.

"It's alright, now go on."

Sophie walked to the closet, grabbed her coat and purse, and headed out the front door. The Sheriff saw Sophie leaving quickly on foot and hustled up behind her

"Mrs. Raney, where are you going?"

Fighting back the tears she turned to him and cried out.

"I'm going back to Poland! They would never leave a woman with four kids in a home without any beds for them to sleep in."

The sheriff turned slightly and saw that Sophie's children were still standing in their front yard clinging to one another watching in horror as their mother appeared to be leaving. The Sheriff stood as his eyes blinked faster and faster trying to fight back the tears at what he was now witnessing.

They are going to leave this poor woman with nothing, not even the simplest of necessities to care for her children, he thought. He yelled out to her.

"Mrs. Raney...please wait...don't go yet. Wait right here." He approached the two men who were in charge, now standing on the front porch.

"Can't you guys just spare the kids beds? Can't you just leave them here? Where are those poor little kids going to sleep? What if this was your mother or your sister?"

Sophie watched the confrontation briefly and turned slowly to continue her walk away from the house.

The Sheriff hurriedly caught up with her from behind and gently put his arm around her small frail shoulders, guiding her back toward the house.

"Mrs. Raney, I've managed to talk them into leaving the beds, I hope this helps."

Tears burst from her eyes as she buried her face into the officer's shoulder. He walked her back to the house.

"Mrs. Raney, is there a chair somewhere that I can get for you?"

"I think down in the basement," she said so quietly they could barely hear her.

"I'll go get that chair...you wait right here."

Soon he returned with an old wooden fold-up chair. He guided the shaking Sophie to sit down.

"I'm going out to talk to your children now. I'll bring them in to you." Silence filled the room as all the men stood still looking at Sophie, her eyes swollen, her small hands clutching onto her purse, sitting in the middle of an empty room. The men looked at each other.

"Hey, we're just doing our job, that's all," one man said to the other quietly as they finished.

SOMEDAY A BLESSING

The intruders finally loaded the last piece of furniture, returned to their vehicles and drove away. Sophie sat, her face cupped in her hands, she started sobbing in total disbelief.

When is this ever going to end? I can't take this anymore. I just don't understand it, God, why, why this now? I just want to die!

Sophie's children soon walked back in the front door, looking at the now desolate home. She looked into their eyes as they all started to weep. They walked into their bedrooms seeing papers, clothes and toys tossed about in the corners. School would be starting soon, but what would they do? They picked up what they could and neatly set things into piles. Folding the clothes that had been thrown out of their dressers, they could not believe the mess the repo men had left. Daryl walked up to Sophie and attempted to comfort her.

"Mom, it's ok, we'll make it...we'll make it..."

All four children soon returned to the living room, handing their mother every bit of change they could scrounge from their bedrooms.

"Here mother," they said. "Here is some money you can use to pay the bills." Sophie grabbed all her children tightly as she cried even harder. She wasn't as alone as she thought she was at that moment in time. Sophie and her kids all snuggled closely together in one of the beds holding each other as they all drifted off to sleep.

The next morning there was yet another knock at the door. It was a man from the electric company.

"Mrs. Raney, we need the full payment on this electric bill or we are going to have to turn your lights off."

Sophie was speechless as she just turned and closed the door behind her. Helpless, she stood staring down the hallway toward her bedroom.

"You son-of-a-bitch you, I hate you! How can you do this to your own children? Just because you divorced me doesn't mean you can do this to them! Everything you are putting me through you're putting your own children through! Don't see that, you fool!" she screamed.

Sophie remained locked up in the house, in shame and in darkness as she waited for the other utility companies to follow suit. She never

145

forgot the comforts and needs of her children. She brought up some old wood crates from the basement, and with a card board box she placed a square piece of ply-board on top of it for a dinner table. She cleaned the house and set things aside the best she could. With canned goods she served cold, she did her best to prepare delicious dinners on her new makeshift table. They had dinner that night by candlelight.

This would be the breaking point for Sophie. She would now need to ask for help, and hoped it would be from someone who was genuinely concerned for her and her children and not just informants for Carl.

Sophie picked up the phone and dialed Grandpa Jeff.

"Dad, I'm going to lose the house. They have come and repossessed all the furniture already. I have been getting letters from the mortgage company. They want three months' payments, and I don't have it. I don't know if I can afford these kids; I don't know what to do. Maybe I should just send the boys to Carl and try and keep the girls and get a small apartment."

Grandpa Jeff responded to Sophie sternly. "No way are you going to split up those kids. You keep them together! I'll come up with the money for the house and will come and get Denise for a while. Don't you give up that house, Sophie. You keep those kids together!"

Sophie lay on her bed that night with worries of becoming a burden on other people. She was a very proud person and so wanted to make it on her own. She hated to ask for help. She tried to fall asleep as she prayed.

I have been through so much God and I have lived, why? Why have I lived? There must be a reason. I'm tired of nothing ever working out for me, always fighting, just to love and be loved. I fear now that my children will be taken. I love them so much, but like everything else in my life, when will they be taken away? I don't understand it, God, why? Why am I being punished for loving something or someone? Why must I lose at everything I do? It's like a roller coaster ride, so slow to the top but yet so fast to get to the bottom. I feel so helpless, like when I topped that hill in front of that

SOMEDAY A BLESSING

prison that day. I saw no way out, I felt so trapped, so helpless and now here I am again, alone! Why? I work and care for my children, just like my father did, all for nothing, always for nothing. When will this all end?

The next morning, another knock on the door brought Sophie and the kids to peek out the window, terrified at what or who they may see now. Standing at their door was their neighbor Bill. She opened the door slowly.

"You need lights?" he asked. "I saw the electric company here. Open your side window, Sophie, and I'll run an extension cord in, at least you can have one light."

Later that same day with a quick knock, the milk man left two gallons of milk on their front porch. Sophie yelled out trying to catch him.

"I don't have the money for this! I didn't order it!"

"I know! Your neighbors down there," he pointed down the street. "The Scott's—they paid for it."

For months to come, every other day two gallons of milk would appear on Sophie's front porch. Even Carl's old boss from Ford Motor Company pulled up in a truck.

"I heard what happened. You need a refrigerator?"

Lonnie and Chuck carried a small gas stove over, knowing Sophie had nothing to cook on. They also strung a water hose from the back of their house over to the bathroom window which was above the bathtub.

"We can fill the bathtub, at least you can have water to wash with and to flush the toilet," they said.

Soon neighbors from all around lined up at the front door, carrying boxes of food, pieces of furniture and clothing. The Raney house came back to life again—piece by piece.

Sophie stood in disbelief as the neighbors who she had thought were all against her were all lining up to help her. For the first time in months, she was not alone. People did care about her and the kids. The next meal was served hot with a small light burning at the end of an extension cord. The Raneys sat around the makeshift table.

147

"You were right, Daryl. We will make it," Sophie said.

Grandpa Jeff called a week later.

"I have sold some cattle. I'm going to pay the past due mortgage payments on your house and I'm sending you the money to turn your utilities back on."

Much to Sophie's surprise, however, Grandpa Jeff not only paid up her mortgage, he had made enough money to pay off the $7,000 note completely!

Sophie went next door to tell Bill he could have his extension cord back and thanked him for all his help. She also told him she would repay him for the electric bill, which he refused. He handed her a cold beer, her first ever. This time no one could tell her not to drink it, which was a demand of the past. After the first few sips, the beer began to warm her veins and a feeling of calm began to overtake her. Carl never allowed Sophie to drink, smoke, or wear make-up, but yet he married a woman who did all those things. It never made sense to her.

The next trip she took to the Milgram's Grocery Store, she walked in to the liquor side of the store. Looking around to make sure there wasn't anyone there she knew, she picked up a six-pack of beer, and turned to leave briskly. Standing behind her was former President Harry S. Truman. Sophie was embarrassed as President Truman nodded toward her, wearing his signature hat. She quietly asked if he remembered her from Crosses Restaurant, where she had been working as a waitress.

"Ah, yes. Sophie, right?"

"Yes!" she said proudly, not believing he actually remembered her. After all, he had been a President of the United States and she was a simple waitress at a small bar and grill. President Truman then covertly handed her a $10 bill while grasping her small hands.

"My wife and I love the food there, very nice place," he said with a nod and a wink as he walked away.

Sophie started working at Cross Tavern and Restaurant in Sugar Creek, Missouri in late 1964. Slowly, she was able to replace her household furnishings and eventually was able to purchase a used

SOMEDAY A BLESSING

vehicle with the tips she made for giving great service. It wasn't long after Sophie began working for the restaurant that she had patrons that would only eat there on the nights she was working and only if she waited on them. Some customers would arrive at the restaurant for dinner and turn to leave when they found out Sophie was off that night. She became extremely popular, with her attractive Polish accent, bubbly personality, and terrific sense of humor. Never once when the Polka was played could she resist stopping whatever she was doing and taking a short dance around the room. For 35 years, she remained working for the restaurant, meeting new friends.

She still spent most of her time keeping the house in order. All bills were paid first. Denise remembered how her mother knew every price of grocery items as she made out her list. She knew the cost right down to the tax. When Sophie earned enough time for vacation, she spent her vacations not on a posh trip, but painting the whole house, trimming and mowing the yard to a golf course appearance.

Sophie worked harder than most people. She remained in the house she had once shared with Carl, however, she continued to battle with the demons inside her. For many years, Sophie worked until 1:00 or 2:00 a.m., three to four nights a week and returned home in the wee hours where her children had put themselves to bed. She would get up in the morning, prepare a quick breakfast for her children, get them off to school, and return to her bed, exhausted, and would sleep until the kids came home from school.

As the Gypsy had predicted, Sophie eventually met another dark-haired man. This one did have wealth and she and Larry were together for 15 years until he passed away. They never married. Everything the Gypsy had predicted had come true in a strange way.

Because she worked at a restaurant and bar, her co-workers always encouraged her to stay after hours for a drink or two. Sophie had been drinking beer occasionally but had never had a "hard" drink until starting her job at Crosse's. The bartender and other waitresses loved to have Sophie stay, tell her jokes as she became increasingly intoxicated. She enjoyed these times, also. It helped her escape from all things passed. Her alcohol addiction haunted her for the rest of her

149

life. Even though alcohol was a crutch for her, she never missed a day of work. The children's clothes and her home were kept spotless, and the pantry was always filled with food.

In 1987, Sophie's two sisters and brother came to America for a two-month visit, a reunion long overdue for the siblings. Tears and laughter filled the Raney house once again. At last, all misunderstanding of the past came to a rest. The unanswered letters, the absence of Sophie all those years, she was able to explain to her sisters and brother why they never heard from her during those tumultuous times. As the years multiplied, it had become increasingly more and more difficult to make that move to contact her family. It was Sophie's daughters who finally decided to locate and contact their mother's family in Poland and made this reunion a reality. With the help of an interpreter, Deborah and Denise were able to locate their long lost relatives in the same place where Sophie was born, long awaiting a word from their sister.

Sophie's battle with her demons continued as age took its toll on her body but never her mind. She leaned on the bottle of alcohol again and again. She could often be found with pictures of her family, Carl, her children spread out on her dining room table where she would sit drinking and crying into the wee hours of the morning. Always wondering, *Why God? Where is my blessing in this life? I've always tried to be a good person. I did what everyone told me, all my life.*

As she held a small scrapbook filled with pictures, letters, and newspaper clippings, only between the lines will one see her blessings. Not given, directed, or instructed, but as one receives it. It could be as small as an electrical cord bringing light into a darkened room, an old used sofa brought up from someone's basement, boxes of hand me downs or warm blankets. Sophie's life may have never been written in the stars as being blessed, but the tools she received through all her pain and sorrows have given the people around her the strength to carry on. Her story lives on in the hearts and souls of all who have met her. Laughter she found in her darkest hours. Courage found in her as bombs fell around her, marching without food for

SOMEDAY A BLESSING

days, never knowing if she would live to see the morning sun rise again.

She looked to the heavens that have prophesied her many prayers and rivers of tears. She walked many man-made paths in her life. Though frail, now she speaks of how she would not change a thing if this was meant to be her destiny. She has loved, had a family, and many blessings great or small. She thanks God everyday for those blessings. She reminisces about all the freedom and material possessions taken from her in her life, but they could never rob her of her laughter, her life here in the United States, or her dreams. She has been defeated, but only for a little while as her strength arose from above, the Lord's voice would call down to her.

"Sit, little one. It will be alright."

As the rain bounces off the window pane, she sits and stares visualizing the coming fog. Her eyes fade into a surreal river; sure-footed she walks along the banks covered in a carpet of green grass. Bending down, she scoops a hand full of cool, clear water. She leans back, dripping it down her forehead. She slowly lowers her head and sees a vision in the swirling water, a room full of people. Standing there are Carl, Peg, Nazi soldiers, ex-lovers, and all who had once tried to destroy her. She thinks for a moment, as she steps further back in time, seeing her father with his accordion on his knee, playing as always every Saturday night. Her mother, brother, and sisters gathered in the kitchen dancing to the cheerful Polka music, so happy, so free. She sighs to herself.

"I will never stop dancing, Father...never."

Looking back at the crowded room, Sophie tips back her head and laughs, "HA HA! I made it!"

...Never stop dancing...

151

Printed in the United States
76142LV00002B/30